# HOUSE & GARDEN'S

# 26 EASY LITTLE GARDENS

**A STUDIO BOOK · THE VIKING PRESS · NEW YORK**

# CONTENTS

Copyright © 1969, 1970, 1971, 1972, 1973, 1974, 1975 by The Condé Nast Publications Inc. All rights reserved. First published in 1975 by The Viking Press, Inc. 625 Madison Avenue, New York, N.Y. 10022. Published simultaneously in Canada by The Macmillan Company of Canada Limited. Printed in U.S.A.

The quotation on page 11 is from *Men and Gardens* by Nan Fairbrother; Copyright © 1956 by Nan Fairbrother and reprinted by kind permission of Alfred A. Knopf, Inc.

The photograph on the endpapers is by Leslie Gill. The other photographs in the book are by Morley Baer (pages 40, 41, 42, and 43), Ernst Beadle (pages 10, 12, 13, 14, 15, 17, 24, 25, 30, 31, 32, 33, 35, 36, 37, 48, 49, 52, 54, 55, 56, 57, 66, 67, 72, 73, 74, 75, 76, 77, 84, 85, 86, 87, 125, and 137), Emerick Bronson (pages 38, 39, 44, 45, 46, and 47), Dean Brown (pages 20, 22, 23, 26, 27, 28, and 29), William Grigsby (pages 60, 61, 62, and 63), Horst P. Horst (pages 50, 51, 64, 65, 68, 69, 70, and 71), Fred Lyon (pages 78 and 79), and Hans Namuth (pages 18, 19, 58, 59, 80, 82, and 83). The garden plans were drawn by Adolph Brotman.

Library of Congress Cataloging in Publication Data
Main entry under title:
House & garden's 26 easy little gardens.
  (A Studio book)
  Includes index.
  1. Gardening. I. House & garden.
SB453.H764    712'.6    75-15700
ISBN 0-670-37979-4

A vest-pocket
salad garden
by a front door

*The garden 22*
*The plan 96*

An organic
vegetable patch
by a
swimming pool

*The garden 24*
*The plan 97*

An enclosed
green garden
with hardy plants
and a tower
for looking out

*The garden 26*
*The plan 98*

This book was edited by
**MARY JANE POOL**
Editor-in-Chief
House & Garden


Written by
**MARYBETH LITTLE WESTON**
Garden Editor


Designed by
**MIKI DENHOF**
Associate Editor

# 7

# 8

# 9

# 10

# 11

*A kitchen yard
of herbs
growing in
wooden boxes*

*The garden 48
The plan 110*

*A green garden
on a city rooftop
where everything
grows in pots*

*The garden 50
The plan 112*

*A well-designed
cutting garden and a
porch garden
of house plants*

*The garden 52
The plan 114*

*A canopy
of cherry trees and
a paisley
flower garden*

*The garden 56
The plan 116*

*A summer
cottage garden
of easy-to-grow
flowers and
climbing roses*

*The garden 58
The plan 118*

A miniature orchard
and berry garden
in boxes
for easy care

22

A patchwork of
little kitchen gardens
growing from a family's
love of cooking

23

A green and white
all-season garden for a
shady city backyard

24

An organic
backyard farm of
fruit trees, vegetables,
and flowers

25

An automated
no-work carpet garden
that never
needs weeding

26

THE GARDENS

"I didn't know the meaning of life until I started to garden," someone quoted to me recently. Watching life and its secrets and surprises in your own garden is a wondrous thing. The joy comes to some very early. For instance, a bursting vegetable garden you'll soon see is the creation of a twenty-year-old.

A garden can be paradise at any age. I asked a friend who has retired to a few green acres by the sea, "Bill, why do you like to garden?" His eyes flashed and he quickly replied, "I don't know, but thank God I do!" Like Fernand Lequenne, who wrote *My Friend the Garden*, he sees in his garden the essence of life. I asked another friend whose garden is growing more glorious each year (his business life is hectic and his family life hyperactive), "Richard, why do you like to garden?" "It's so peaceful," he said, smiling, "and the flowers don't talk back." One of the gardeners in this book confided about her garden, "I am restored by its little bit of order in a disorderly world. Even weeding and grooming are soothing. In a little garden work is pleasant because there is not too much of it."

The little gardens collected here are small works of nature helped along by men, women, and children of many inclinations and every occupation. Each garden has been conceived, planted, and dug into for a variety of reasons and in a variety of places—city, suburbs, and deep country. Many are just for weekend pleasure of one sort or another. All have appeared in House & Garden. It was Alexander Liberman, our Editorial Director, who first suggested doing a series of "very personal gardens." We were in the Art Department looking at photographs Horst had taken of his

*The shapes we make for ourselves are geometrical, and the background of civilized life is more or less rectangular. Our rooms and houses are arrangements of cubes, our doors and windows, furniture and rugs, books and boxes—all their angles are right angles and all their sides are straight. . . . This geometrical setting of our urban lives has its own beauty. . . . But still we miss the shapes of growing things which we have lived with for a million years. We fill our rooms with flowers and plants, we set our cities with trees and green gardens, we use the shapes of vegetable life to humanize our geometric abstractions. . . . For man has a natural sympathy for the background of green life which surrounds him; all people have taken pleasure in trees and flowers, and the story of Eden was invented to explain a love of gardens as old as Adam.*

Nan Fairbrother
*Men and Gardens*

11

own garden. Horst's was the first published of what we refer to as "possible gardens," gardens that are easy enough for one person to take care of.

We are showing some of the smallest, numbered one to twenty-six, and they've been chosen for almost as many reasons.

Gardens for herbs, for flowers, for fragrance. A garden for a place to entertain. A garden to look at. A garden to bring the country to the city. A garden for color. A garden to enjoy all seasons. A garden to produce fruits and vegetables for the table. An organic garden for health. A garden for rest. A garden for eating out of doors. A cutting garden. A garden that's portable. A garden that's an unroofed extension of the house. A garden as art. A garden for walking. A garden to welcome friends.

Full of inspiration and ideas for even the never-before gardener, each garden is shown in color with an explanation of what the owner wanted it to be. To learn more about any one of them, turn to the corresponding number at the back. You will find what you need to know to guide you to a similar success—a detailed plan, simple "how-to" suggestions, and a plant list. From all the garden experiences in this book, you see that in a runaway world a garden is a lovely place to slow down and feel the gentle rhythm of life. A garden can be a sure route to happiness for almost everyone.

Mary Jane Pool
*Editor-in-Chief*
*House & Garden*

*Painting a house with a fresh coat of flowers does wonders. Plants can make a porch, deck, balcony, or street a happier place to be and to see.*

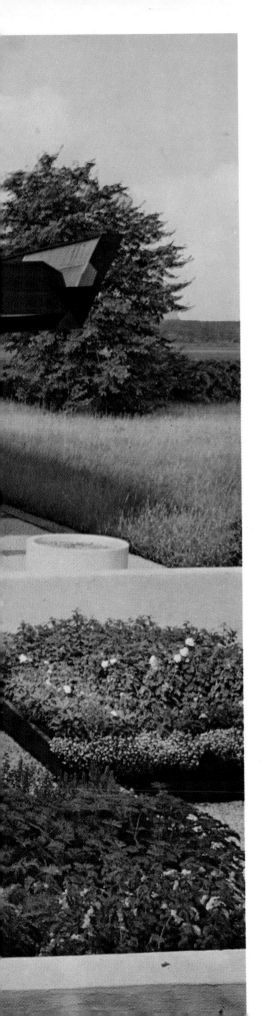

**A small
walled garden
set in a field of
wildflowers**

On a snowy day one February, magazine editor Babs
Simpson was thinking summer thoughts. She wrote a
note to a friend, imagining for her house "a small formal
garden surrounded by wildflowers, with a tall poppy
leaning over the wall." She wanted "herbs for the
kitchen, flowers for the house, fragrance in the air," but
did not want the rabbits to get there first. By late June
her garden had grown from mindscape to landscape.

15

Photographed as it looked in its first summer, Mrs. Simpson's 22-by-44-foot garden is lapped by a field of wild native grasses and wildflowers. It was sunken to preserve the view from the house and walled to keep out wind and weeds. Of painted concrete, the wall is 22 inches on the outside, "higher than a rabbit can jump, or at least higher than Long Island rabbits jump." A center bed contains herbs and scented geraniums. Flowers for fragrance and for cutting grow in beds along the walls. The flower palette is primarily white, lavender, and blue, miming the white and blue paths and the sky. At each end is a hardy orange tree, "terribly pretty, with an almost medieval look." An espaliered pear was planted against the side of the house. "This is the working garden I wanted, easy to maintain. But what I love most is the serenity that comes from just opening the gate." Because of its precisionist pattern by landscape designer Judith Heller, the garden is attractive even in winter. "But isn't it maddening to have to wait for spring?" asks Mrs. Simpson, her head full of ideas for another year's flowers and herbs.

## 2 A front-walk garden that says welcome with old-fashioned flowers, evergreen ground covers

For fifty years Mrs. Louis B. Bock's perennial garden has charmed guests and passersby. Slowing down for a glimpse of it through the wisteria-arched gateway is second nature to Long Island motorists who have come to think of it as summer's first hello and last good-by. From the picket fence to the holly-framed porch, her flowers bloom in cumulous drifts of lavender, pink, and blue each May, then white, blue, and red until frost. They are like reliable old friends, and "people tell me they enjoy seeing them each year, too."

This landlocked scallop is small and makes minimal demands, yet it offers choice evergreen and evergray plants for year-round pattern, fresh strawberries to savor, fragrant herbs to sniff or to snip for cooking, low walls for sitting in the sun, even a scallop-shell birdbath to amuse the eye. Frances Ferguson's Connecticut garden by a driveway has far more impact than size. The center path is just 20 feet long, and the perimeter is 40 feet. The landscape architect: Eloise A. Ray.

**3 A scallop shell garden with fluted rows of easy-care herbs**

A garden that looks good enough to eat, and is, borders New York cookbook writer Robert Ackart's driveway and front path. Like three salad bowls, three beds are crisp with a variety of lettuce, chives and other herbs, strawberries, small tomatoes, a sun shower of marigolds—a delicious way to welcome dinner guests and to keep harvests easy.

4 **A vest-pocket
salad garden
by a front door**

# 5

**An organic vegetable patch by a swimming pool**

A shady backyard with a pool in the only sunny corner left college student Kirk Beckwith very little room for the organic garden he wanted to grow during his summer at home in Connecticut. He decided to stake out a 20-foot strip between pool and evergreens, and stretched it tall with 12-foot sunflowers. He put down a grass-clipping mulch and planted marigolds and nasturtiums as pest-deterring companion plants, a sort of poolside buddy system to safeguard his summer crops.

6 To create a green garden is an achievement, especially in the dry Texas hill country where architect Albert Keidel lives. He even succeeded in walling out wildlife without walling out the view.

**An enclosed green garden with hardy plants and a tower for looking out**

27

Deer still play in the flinty wilderness around this ranch house, and native evergreens are scarce, except for live oaks that stay green through drought and winter wind. Mr. Keidel wanted a transition from raw land to front door, with a small lawn to take care of but a place for entertaining.

In this fenced garden of hedges and hardy plants, perhaps the most triumphal leap is the lookout tower. Part gazebo, part Spanish mirador, part treehouse, it has second-story benches for musicians at a party, or for being blissfully alone. To get there, you climb a ladder you can pull up if you choose.

7 **A vertical garden on a city terrace, a leafy path in the sky** With more zest than space for gardening, photographer Ernst Beadle made his city terrace a vertical garden that goes right up the wall and spills from arbors and fences. He designed wall-hugging habitats for caladiums, vines, rock plants, roses, herbs, bulbs, trees.

"This is a very concentrated little garden," Mr. Beadle says, with some understatement. His penthouse walkway is just 9 feet at its widest. The garden grows on brick walls, wood shelves, wire trellises and racks, even in a barrel and around salvaged city art. Roses bloom six months of the year squeezed in redwood boxes. "Roses are real urban characters and thrive on city air." A desire for rock plants eighteen

stories up inspired his 10-foot obelisk. In canted shelves, *Sedum spectabile* at the top (a burst of rose-pink when it blooms), pale blue harebells, and other enchanting rock plants grow as happily as if in mountain crevices. Cucumber vines and Concord grapes hang from fences along the parapet, and tomatoes stretch 8 feet upward on strings. The once-bleak walkway is now a garden path in the sky.

*1. Terrace with benches, roses, and a morning-glory arbor built to block out a water tank. 2. Pittosporum, fancy-leaf geraniums, rue, and other plants chosen for beauty of leaf. 3. Scented geraniums on wire fern rack. 4. Roses and skyline. 5. Awning area for shade-loving plants and guests. Planter with frog serves as lily pond. 6. Portulaca in a barrel; parsley, basil. 7. Coney Island lion among elephant's ears, flowers, and ferns.*

When Jack and Esther Larson were first married, they were given an herb cookbook and decided that their first garden, someday, would surely be an herb garden. When they bought a 1770 farmhouse, they set about planting a kitchen garden by the front porch. As if fragrant lilac and wisteria were not enough to enchant any visitor, the dooryard garden, only about 12 by 22 feet, has a flagstone path, and a picket fence with climbing strawberries. Steppingstones are lapped by thyme. In spring the hardy herbs that sleep through winter under snow perk up and leaf and bloom another year. Tender bay trees and twelve-year-old rosemaries are moved outdoors in their pots. This garden is fragrant to sit by, especially in rain under the shelter of the porch, or to walk by on the way to the front door. And always at the Larsons', the kitchen is fragrant with fresh and dried culinary herbs and all-season herbal bouquets.

 **A dooryard of fragrant herbs and a walk-through herb garden in a meadow**

From the top of a green slope of mingled grass and thyme, one can see the formal brick paths that are part of the asymmetrical plan of this garden. It is a maze of herb beds, each one different. Two chairs are all but hidden in the borders. Outside, by a stone path, are starworts such as asters, feverfew, and pot marigolds.

## A dooryard of fragrant herbs and a walk-through herb garden in a meadow

By definition, an herb garden is a useful garden—useful for flavor, fragrance, medicine, dyes, and quotable lore and legends. For their second herb garden, in a meadow behind their house, the Larsons collected all manner of pretty and useful plants, including fruits. It is enclosed by a rail fence and, as in medieval herb gardens, by sweet eglantine roses. All of the seventy-odd plants they grow have a long history of kitchen use or as cures and charms. The garden is an irresistible place for gatherers, chipmunks and guests alike, but "herbs are prolific and there is enough for all." The Larsons were helped in their learning and planning by a good neighbor, the Connecticut herb grower Adelma G. Simmons, whom they discovered first through her books.

# 9

## A small green garden with a lilac walk

This jewel box of a garden offers Laura Bishop the serenity of unchanging green and the joy of experimentation. Like nested green boxes, an evergreen yew hedge frames borders of lilac-dotted evergreen vinca, framing evergreen boxwood. The crisscrossed boxwood, in a bed 10 by 20 feet, has flowers that can change with the Connecticut seasons.

Fog, sun, and salt wind shaped the Monterey cypresses, rarest of North American trees, that stand guard over actress Jean Arthur's house. The garden is bounded by a pulsing California highway, yet when you walk through the torii-like gate, you are in another world. In this place of whispering treetops you whisper, too. Everywhere there is something serene to contemplate—something green and growing, something tranquil and timeless.

**A whispering garden in the Japanese manner, enclosed for serenity**

In the Japanese manner, a fence encloses a mosslike lawn, wind-sculpted trees, and a reflecting pool with stepping-stones. A dry landscape garden in the Zen tradition is cloistered in Miss Arthur's house and seen only from a bedroom and adjoining plant room, when shoji panels slide apart. The statue is of Kwannon, goddess of mercy, who is known in China as Kuan Yin.

## A casual riverside garden with her perennials, his rock plants

A casual garden at its best shows what an unstinting landscaper nature can be. Allowing for nature's own quirks helps Dr. and Mrs. Louis Wardell make the most of a riverbank. A dry rock wall is his, a moist slope is hers, and nature's way is theirs.

The woodland river gliding and cascading past their house provides water for the rock garden, the flower-stippled slope with clematis, peonies, and poppies near an old well, hosta growing as a centerpiece in a millstone table, geraniums on a terrace.

*To buttress a wild bank across from their Connecticut house, the Wardells added ferns and day lilies—"They have roots like building blocks"—to native plants already there. After experimenting to learn what perennials could take the dampness of the slope, Mrs. Wardell recommends primulas, Japanese iris, columbine, forget-me-nots, campanula, foxglove, lythrum, astilbe, and monkshood.*

# 12 A kitchen yard of herbs growing in wooden boxes

The Frank MacGregor Smiths did not expect to find a garden when they went to an antiques show a few years ago. But there it was: a green and pewter-gray herb display in weathered wood boxes, a practical idea for terrace or city rooftop, and perfect for the stony 13-by-20-foot kitchen yard behind their suburban New York house. "Completely captivated," they sought out the designer Adelma G. Simmons, and "the upshot is that we bought the fence, boxes, and herbs outright and have enjoyed them ever since." A bed with a sundial on a stump grows only culinary herbs. The one behind it has decorative herbs, and so do the narrow boxes framing the paths. In a building behind their house the Smiths dry herbs.

To walk into the welcome of a green garden is a happy way for a city day to begin or end. Green thoughts in green shade make this garden restful for Ken Scott, a designer from Indiana whose fabrics are made in Milan. He resurfaced a tarred rooftop with decking and painted it and a metal shelter green. Everything here grows in terra-cotta pots—the ivy on the walls, tree roses, annuals. He is a renter, so even the deck is movable.

## 13 A green garden on a city rooftop where everything grows in pots

Thalassa Cruso's encouraging and humorous approach to gardening—"my notion is not to be bullied too much by my plants"—has made her own garden thrive and her converts to gardening multiply. An author and television personality (*Making Things Grow*), she uses her old-fashioned house on Cape Cod as an idea workshop as well as a place for family holidays. For her cutting garden, she and her husband, archaeologist Hugh Hencken, simplified an old garden enclosed by a privet hedge. It had been a big vegetable garden when their three children were growing up, a formal rose garden before that, and is now "a flower garden with elbow-room." Grass panels and stone paths invite strolling. Mulched walkways separate each curved ribbon of flowers and keep them manageable and almost weed-free. From the unfussy pergola to the gateway, perennials and annuals are staged in a crescendo of height and color and provide bloom all season. A low birdbath, sculpture, and a few choice evergreens provide winter interest.

# 14
**A well-designed
cutting garden
and a porch garden
of house plants**

A summer porch garden of house plants has shade for ferns. Planks of sun-loving succulents, rooted in sphagnum moss, are portable. Begonias, geraniums, hydrangeas, and other plants are staged on steps in an alcove, bask in morning sun and under fluorescent lights that extend the day and make up for cloudy ones. A plastic overhang diverts pelting rain.

54

Under a spring canopy of pink cherry blossoms, the Thomas B. Hesses can enjoy lunch by the swimming pool and a vantage point on Connecticut countryside. Japanese flowering cherries grafted to trunks of ordinary upright cherries are set 10 feet apart and tied to form dense arcs. For the sunny cutting garden Mrs. Hess wanted an interesting place both to walk in and to cut in. An old corral became a paisley pattern of looping paths and curving flower beds. Peonies, roses, and clematis have their own beds. Tulips brighten the garden in spring, annuals take over in summer, and chrysanthemums open in fall. The Hesses' house plants take a holiday outdoors in summer. Landscape architect: James Fanning.

**A canopy of cherry trees and a paisley flower garden**

75

# 16

**A summer cottage garden of easy-to-grow flowers and climbing roses**

Ocean winds dishevel the fields around the house where Robert Dash lives on Long Island. So instead of trying to surround his cottage with flowers, he sensibly surrounded flowers with a cottage. Gales shake his roses, tumble the garden's heavy metal benches, but the plants survive. Dash, a painter who wanted "a garden full of easy flowers that look as if they got together and did it all themselves," says that even if it looks unstudied, "a garden is planned like a painting, though the texture and color intervals keep changing."

# 17 A move-around garden that flowers wherever you put it

Plants in pots can change a garden overnight or be moved indoors if there is a change of plans or weather. Mrs. Enid A. Haupt varies her terrace to please the eye and please the plant. Begonias, echeverias, and other pot plants make instant borders.

Her portable pot plants confined to a few small areas are the only splash of color in Mrs. Haupt's view of Long Island Sound. A brick ledge under wide, shady eaves keeps a three-tiered flower garden on view on both sides of wide windows. A move-around garden that flowers where you put it is always at its peak. Dormant or spent plants can recover out of sight. Moving plants to suitable spots in summer also helps keep them strong and healthy. Mrs. Haupt says, "A flower in a pot, rather than in a vase, truly brings a garden indoors. You <u>see</u> the cycle of life, the wonder of nature."

*Only the shade-loving fuchsias and sun-loving echeverias (the succulents that look like sculptured jade roses) stay outside all season. Tuberous begonias go in on special occasions, cool off each night outdoors. The changeable three-tiered garden has begonias in baskets, tall fuchsia standards, pots of geraniums, and tubbed ficus trees (F. retusa nitida)* with succulents in small pots at their feet.

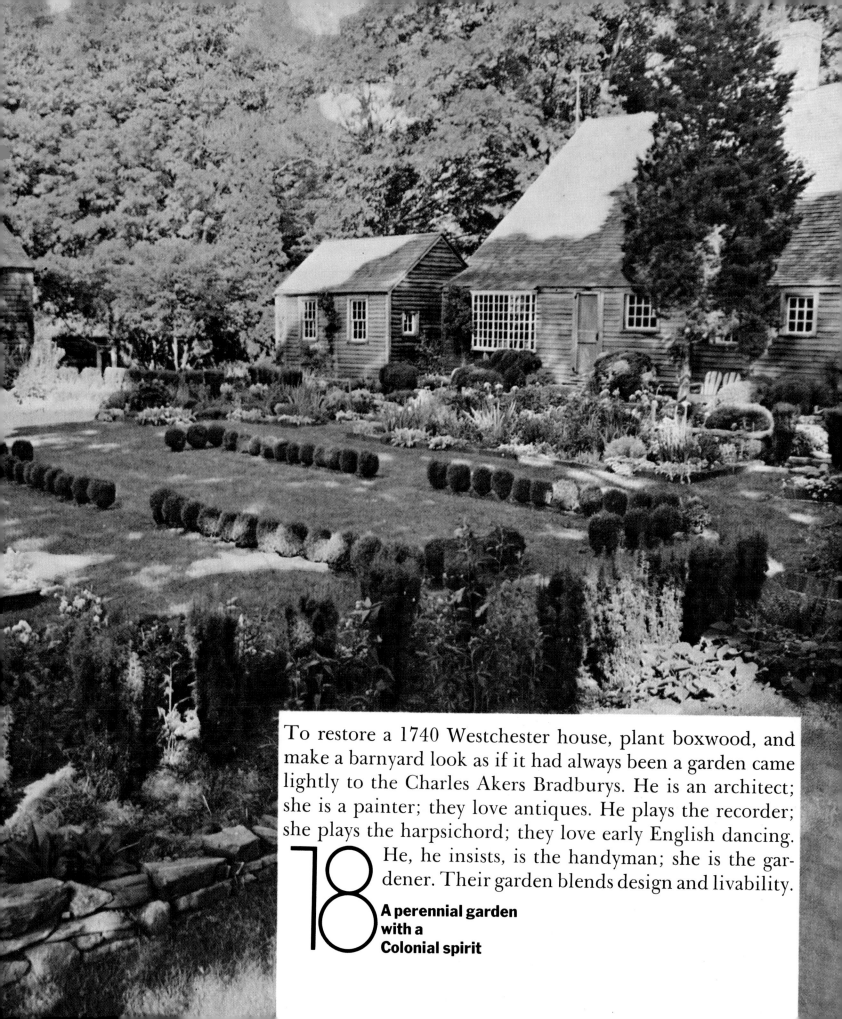

To restore a 1740 Westchester house, plant boxwood, and make a barnyard look as if it had always been a garden came lightly to the Charles Akers Bradburys. He is an architect; she is a painter; they love antiques. He plays the recorder; she plays the harpsichord; they love early English dancing. He, he insists, is the handyman; she is the gardener. Their garden blends design and livability.

**78**

**A perennial garden
with a
Colonial spirit**

"This garden has flowers, vegetables, and herbs. It needs no spraying, no chemical fertilizers, no cultivation, and no watering if the rain gauge on the fence has an inch of good news." For Harry Rogers, who gardens in Connecticut only on weekends, an organic garden with a labor-saving hay mulch is the answer. He uses bottomless wine jugs as miniature greenhouses for seedlings.

# 79

**A weekender's easy-does-it organic hay-mulch vegetable garden**

# 20 Pot luck: portable plants for sunny and shady terraces

Horst, with his artist's eye and camera, has recorded many of the great gardens of the world. But as a dedicated gardener himself, he has an unusual problem. From April to fall, just when there is everything to do and so much in bloom to enjoy, he is often traveling to other people's gardens. At home intermittently, he has learned to be philosophical, to welcome whatever grows—"As one gets older there are fewer and fewer plants one doesn't like"—and to depend on, and make the best of, plants for sale at roadside stands. Many of his effects are frankly impromptu, the result of instant potting or transplanting moments after he gets home or before the arrival of Sunday lunch guests. Roses in pots, and petunias in hanging baskets, join his hibiscus and other flowers under a pergola, his summer living room. It faces a grass terrace framed by boxed spruces.

Coleus and tuberous begonias, some in pots, illumine a shady walkway of carefree impatiens, vinca, and ferns. Path in spring has native violets and lily of the valley moved from

Small terraces, courtyards, and walkways rim Horst's one-story house, and a movable feast of flowers turns them into gardens always at their best when he is there. In a bedroom terrace that catches morning sun, he plants pot-luck tulips or primulas in spring, gloxinias and sedum in summer, chrysanthemums in fall. Queen Elizabeth roses in containers are purchased each summer, then planted in fall in a cutting garden with the other roses of summers past. Green-and-red coleus makes an inviting transition from pink brick steps to a shady green lawn. The rest of Horst's Long Island garden is planned to survive his absence—evergreens, wildflowers, easy perennials, flowering shrubs.

nearby woods. Mr. Horst left mossy holes in a brick terrace for potting or planting flowers in season. Portable grandiflora roses bring summer to the awninged doorway of a guest wing.

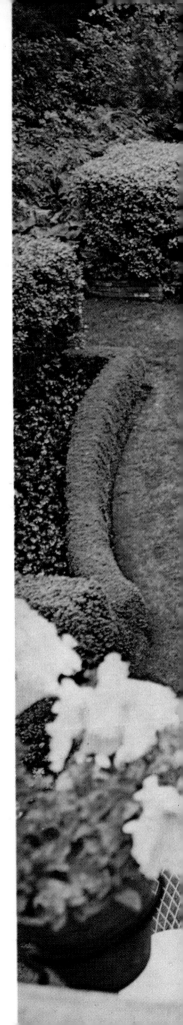

Beauty continually renewed is one of the deep satisfactions of gardening. To propagate one house plant or evergreen so that it becomes many, to start with a raw clearing and keep working until you have several small linked gardens, are arts and pleasures Mr. and Mrs. J. Liddon Pennock, Jr., have shared since they were newlyweds. The first garden they wrested from woodland behind their house near Philadelphia is a green circle in a square adjoining their terrace. For years it was self-contained. Then they built another round garden, with a lily pond and concentric circles of greenery, and linked the two with ivy-ribboned steps. Little by little they built other small gardens.

# 21 A perfectionist's small round gardens and green-thumb pot-plant ideas

Recalling childhood holidays "in France, where even the great houses had intimate gardens," Mrs. Quaintance Mason remodeled farm buildings in Westchester, New York, and planted a small orchard in a gravel courtyard. Dwarf apples, pears, peaches, and crabapples flourish in boxes, brimming with strawberries and open at the bottom. Raspberries grow in low boxes by a fence. Bee skeps, a dovecote, and white roses add charm.

## 22 A miniature orchard and berry garden in boxes for easy care

A calico patchwork of small vegetable gardens, each edged with flowers, grows on New England farmland by the sea. Everyone in the Josiah H. Child, Jr., family is involved in it—growing, picking, cooking, sometimes just walking to enjoy the pleasing design. Short rows are seeded all season for continuous easy harvests. Vegetables are picked small for superior taste and texture. The garden began as one tiny trial patch.

**A patchwork of
little kitchen gardens
growing from a family's
love of cooking**

23

Painter Ralph Du Casse lives in a San Francisco town house that originally had no garden, only a dirt slope, behind it. To insure a handsome view from rooms above and to provide privacy, a garden was designed that also overcomes a common handicap of hemmed-in city backyards—shade. A parterre of boxwood spheres and hedges is always green in the courtyard of pink basket-weave brick. A lattice fence, pleached pittosporum trees, and English ivy enfold it. Container-grown white flowers are set in white urns at two corners of the parterre and change with the season. These are lily of the Nile. Landscape architect: Charles Deaton.

## 24 A green and white all-season garden for a shady city backyard

# 25

**An organic backyard farm of fruit trees, vegetables, and flowers**

Many flowers, herbs, vegetables, berries, grapes, fruits, and still a sense of open space are the surprises of this backyard. An organic garden, planned for spare-time care, is bountiful despite limited space, sun, and time. Gardener is Barbara Cagiati Draper, a painter.

This was not a large plot, and it already had a lot on it—house, pump house, barn, shady maples. In an area that gets sun much of the day, Barbara Cagiati Draper made 8-foot gardens, each with a dwarf fruit tree knee-deep in flowers. Vegetables, grapes, and other fruits, combined with herbs and flowers, grow near the barn. Plants are combined to save space and because some help each other. Onions, marigolds, and nasturtiums, she finds, are pungent companion plants that help keep other plants healthy.

This organic gardener does not spray even her miniature orchard or roses. The six fruit trees are underplanted with herbs, bulbs, a rose bush, a profusion of flowers rimmed and raised with railroad ties. By late summer the trees are weighted with apples, pears, and peaches. Grafted to dwarfing rootstock, the trees yield full-size fruit but stay short and easy for one person to prune and harvest.

# 26 An automated no-work carpet garden that never needs weeding

How to have a beautiful garden "without doing any work, especially weeding and hoeing," was solved for the George R. Numrich, Jrs., when a wild idea occurred to Mr. Numrich at a carpeted restaurant: "Maybe outdoor carpet would make an ideal vegetable garden mulch. It's weedproof, verminproof, doesn't mildew. Water runs through it, paths would stay dry, and the ground would hold moisture and heat. If we used a bright color, it might reflect light and promote growth." That spring they rotary-tilled a trial garden, rolled out an unbacked polypropylene carpet, and cut openings to plant in. It so outproduced their dirt garden that next year they carpeted it, too.

85

Just about everything in this carpet garden is automated but the harvest. Peat-pot transplants and large seeds are set in holes made by a 3-inch circular saw attachment on an electric hand drill. Spills are cleaned up by a vacuum or broom. For root crops and fine seeds, 2-inch-wide slits are made with a sharp knife. Slits ease the harvest even of 6-inch onions, a necessity that the Numriches overlooked in the first garden. A bed for perennials—asparagus and rhubarb—dates back to dirt-gardening days and was simply edged by carpet strips. Every morning a standing sprinkler controlled by a timer waters the garden, unless there is a heavy rain. Soluble fertilizer goes through the sprinkler and a gadget linking faucet, tube, and pail.

The unbacked outdoor carpet has a summer border of marigolds, ornamental kale, and cabbage. For the table the Numriches grow Red Acre and Gold Acre cabbage in their upstate New York garden. The carpet will last for years. Crops will rotate to other openings in carefree summers to come.

THE PLANS

**A small walled garden set in a field of wildflowers** was what Babs Simpson wanted. Gales can blow and rabbits can run, but easy-to-maintain flowers and herbs flourish safe from harm. Three steps lead from the gate to blue-stone and marble chip paths. The redwood gate, like the bed retainers in the sunken garden, has a black protective stain matching the trim of the house. Windows and terrace look out on the formality of the little garden and the wildness of the meadow. Here there is no lawn to mow, or need for one.

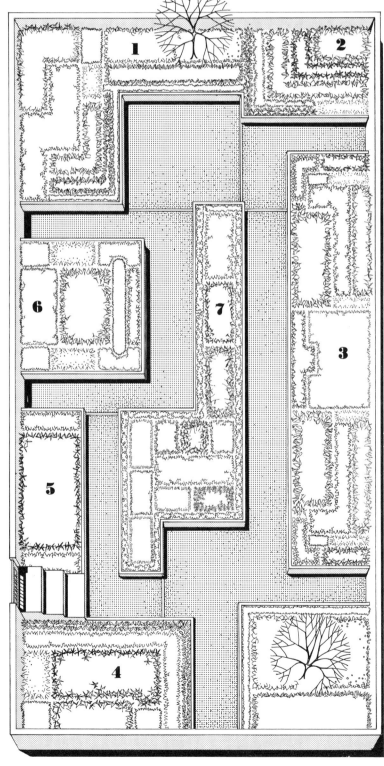

*The garden is 22 by 44 feet. The wall is concrete coated with white marine paint. It is rabbitproof, 22 inches high on the outside. Beds are raised for visual interest and convenience.*

"Simplicity is my aim," this gardener says. Even her plan has geometric clarity, and sturdy long-season plants predominate. Watering is done by a hose and sprinkler, attached to a timer. The bed retainers were filled originally with commercially sterilized soil, plus peat moss, sand, and slow-release organic nutrients. Fine compost is added spring and fall. A winter mulch of salt hay protects perennials through frosts and thaws and is removed in spring. Densely planted the first year, the garden now has simpler blocks of white, lavender, and blue flowers.

*THE PLAN*
1. *Hardy orange tree* (Poncirus trifoliata) *bedded with violets, verbenas, pansies, edged with white sweet alyssum. Mrs. Simpson now grows just easy blue browallia, an annual, edged by gray santolina* (S. chamaecyparissus) .
2. *White petunias and phlox, White Champion lily, Pink Champion lily, blue browallia, edged by white sweet alyssum.*
3. *White petunias and nicotiana, Hidcote lavender* (Lavandula vera) , *gray santolina, lilies. Now blue petunias, lavender, blue lobelia* (L. erinus compacta) , *and campanula* (C. carpatica) .
4. *White phlox, stock, violets. Now white lilies, blue Frikartii asters, blue-leaved rue* (Ruta graveolens) , *and silver-leaved dianthus* (D. allwoodii) .
5. *White phlox, lilies, violets, dianthus, and delphiniums* (Belladonna, Bellamosa, and Casa Blanca) .
6. *White nicotiana and petunias, dianthus, lavender. New addition: a sky-reflecting square birdbath surrounded by lavender with two stands of white cosmos.*
7. *Center herb bed: basil* (sweet, dwarf, and Dark Opal) , *parsley* (flat Italian and curly) , *sage, rosemary, thyme, chives and garlic chives, tarragon, chervil, dill, sweet marjoram, lemon verbena, and garden rocket—also called roquette and rugola* (Eruca sativa) . *Also scented geraniums* (Pelargonium) : *rose, lemon, orange, apple, nutmeg, ginger.*

Surrounding this Long Island house and walled garden is an open field with bordering woodland. Mrs. Simpson pulls up milkweed and ragweed whenever she sees them. She also has the field mowed each fall by tractor to prevent briers and brambles from taking over, but this is done only after the wildflowers have been allowed to go to seed. By skipping the chore of raking, she lets the leavings stay on as a thin mulch, and the flowers replenish themselves. There is now a profusion of daisies, black-eyed Susans, gaillardia, oenothera, chicory, coreopsis, bouncing Bet, butterfly weed. Mrs. Simpson feeds and waters wild birds in return for the seeds they carry here. Poppies, despite many efforts to naturalize them, have refused to prosper, but white narcissus bulbs planted in the field have increased each year: Cheerfulness, Thalia, and Pheasant's Eye.

Perhaps the nicest way to welcome friends is with flowers, especially a linear bouquet running straight to a front door. Mrs. Louis B. Bock's gate is arched by wisteria and her path bordered by perennial flowers and greenery. For half a century, they have welcomed guests and refreshed passers-by. The flowers have multiplied, been divided, but have scarcely been added to in all these many years.

## 2 A front-walk garden that says welcome with old-fashioned flowers, evergreen ground covers

It can be said of perennials, as of postmen, that "neither snow nor rain nor heat nor gloom of night stays these couriers from the swift completion of their appointed rounds," though happily perennials' completion of their rounds is not so swift as reliable. They return faithfully each year with the season's greetings. Mrs. Bock's list of perennials is unusual in that it contains many best known for their leaves and does not contain such popular flowers as peonies, bearded iris, asters, chrysanthemums. The garden is unusual, too, in that it is heavily shaded. When the borders were planted fifty years ago, the trees were not so tall, but here the perennials are accommodating. Even when not in bloom, the front-walk garden is attractive because of the foliage texture. Mrs. Bock long ago exiled any flowers with foliage "that seemed a little coarse." Besides pachysandra and ferns, she has at least a dozen varieties of hosta (also known as funkia or plantain lily), which produce clumps of leaves, often variegated, every year. The collection includes *Hosta caerulea, H. decorata, H. lancifolia, H. plantaginea, H. grandiflora* (jasmine-scented, and a favorite), *H. undulata,* and others. In addition, vines paint the gate, house, and garage with fresh new leaves each spring—Chinese wisteria on the gateposts, Boston ivy on the house, honeysuckle and sweet autumn clematis (*C. paniculata*) on the garage.

Mrs. Bock speaks of each plant by its Latin name. "Botanical names are exact and the language you have in common with garden lovers anywhere in the world." Her advice is as direct as her garden is subtle. To feed and mulch perennials: "We cover them with a ton of manure every winter." For beautiful phlox, one of her specialties: "Cut the blossoms off quickly so they won't set seed." As for planting and dividing: "I'm a little unorthodox, but spring and fall are the times usually observed for these jobs."

*THE PLANTS*
*Artemisia Silver King* (A. albula)
*Astilbe Peach Blossom*
*Bee balm, Horsemint* (Monarda didyma, M. kalmiana, M. salmonea)
*Bellflower* (Campanula latifolia, C. persicifolia, C. rapunculoides, C. rotundifolia)
*Bleeding heart* (Dicentra eximia, D. spectabilis)
*Blue salvia* (S. farinacea)
*Columbine* (Aquilegia, var.)

*Coralbells* (Heuchera sanguinea)
*Day lilies* (Hemerocallis citrina, H. flava)
*Evening primrose* (Oenothera)
*Japanese iris* (I. kaempferi)
*Loosestrife* (Lysimachia clethroides)
*Meadow rue* (Thalictrum adiantifolium, T. aquilegifolium, T. dipterocarpum, T. glaucum)
*Meadowsweet* (Spiraea filipendula hexapetala, S. ulmaria)
*Phlox* (P. carolina, P. paniculata

sieboldii; *annual* P. drummondii)
*Rose campion* (Lychnis coronaria)
*Snakeroot* (Cimicifuga racemosa, C. simplex)
*Statice* (Limonium sinuatum)
*Stonecrop* (Sedum spectabile)
*Sweet cicely* (Myrrhis odorata)
*Sweet rocket* (Hesperis matronalis)
*Valerian* (Valeriana centranthus)
*Veronica* (V. maritima subsessilis, V. spicata, V. virginica)

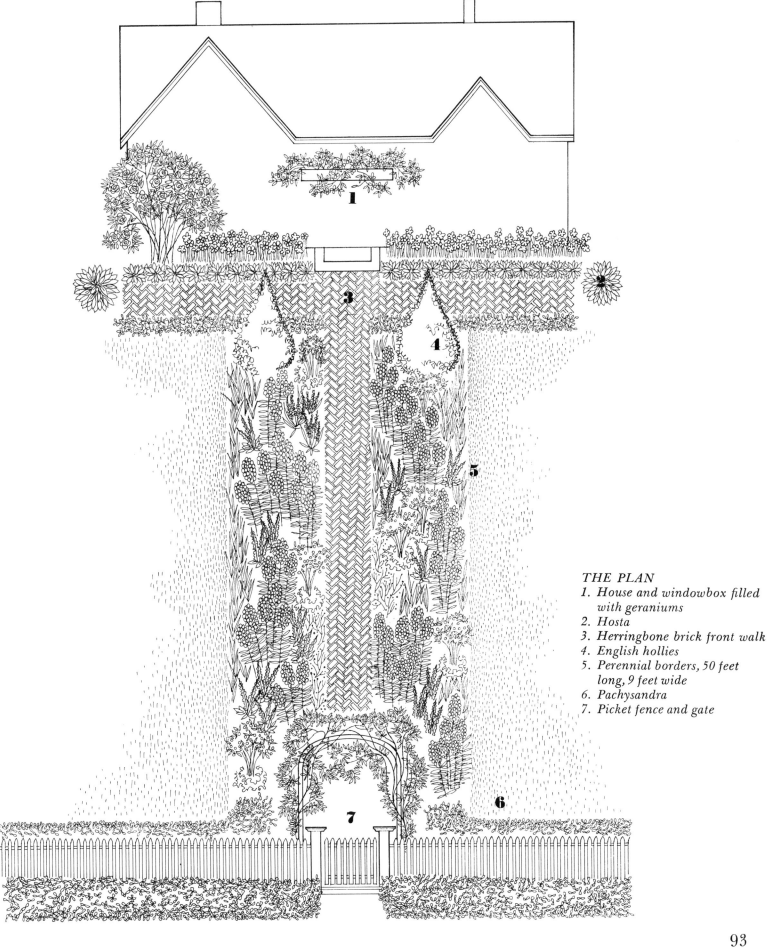

*THE PLAN*
1. *House and windowbox filled with geraniums*
2. *Hosta*
3. *Herringbone brick front walk*
4. *English hollies*
5. *Perennial borders, 50 feet long, 9 feet wide*
6. *Pachysandra*
7. *Picket fence and gate*

93

**3** To replace a triangle of unwilling grass, confined by driveway and trees, Frances Ferguson wanted something interesting to look at and easy to care for. She consulted Eloise A. Ray, a landscape architect in Westport, Connecticut, who believes in letting the land have its say. The land was a sloping, fanlike wedge, and from this the idea of a scallop shell evolved. Green and gray herbs form the fluting and provide flavorful additions to meals and their pastel blossoms in season.

## A scallop shell garden with fluted rows of easy-care herbs

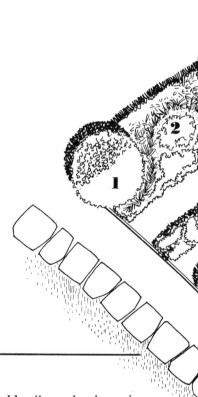

*TO PLANT
A STRAWBERRY JAR*

like the one (10.) Miss Ferguson uses for sempervivum, try this method for good drainage: In the center insert a cardboard cylinder roughly as long as the jar is tall and 3 inches in diameter. Fill it with grit. Add soil or planting mix around this. Remove cardboard to leave a permanent core of grit. Tuck plants in the outside pockets of the jar and around the edge of the top. Sprinkle when the garden is watered. This method also works well for most herbs as well as succulents. For strawberries and other plants that may want a more steady supply of moisture: Insert a cylinder of chicken wire stuffed with wet sphagnum moss and leave it there. Add soil or planting mix around it. Water just the sphagnum so moisture will gradually seep from the moss and the soil will not be disturbed. Still another method: Cut a strip of old garden hose. Perforate it with an icepick or a nail. Stand it upright in the strawberry jar and put a bottle cap on the top end. Add soil or planting mix around it. Remove cap to fill hose with water. Replace cap between waterings. Put a strawberry jar in a garage or other cool place in winter if there is danger of freezing and cracking. Sprinkle occasionally. Some gardeners have success growing herbs and succulents as winter house plants in strawberry jars.

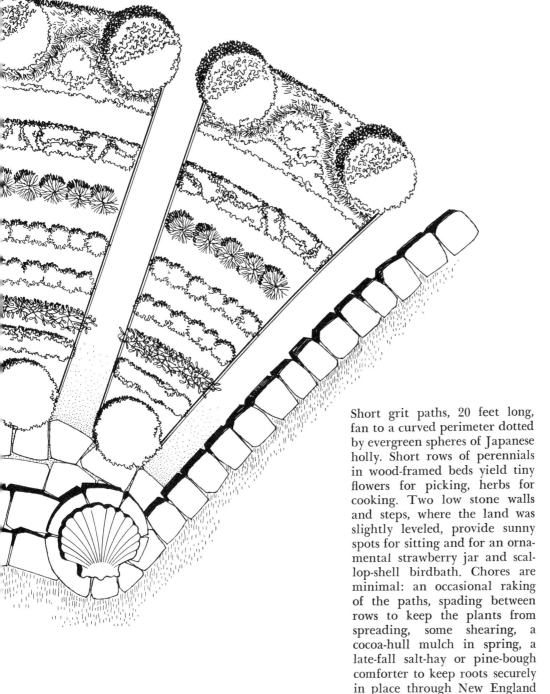

Short grit paths, 20 feet long, fan to a curved perimeter dotted by evergreen spheres of Japanese holly. Short rows of perennials in wood-framed beds yield tiny flowers for picking, herbs for cooking. Two low stone walls and steps, where the land was slightly leveled, provide sunny spots for sitting and for an ornamental strawberry jar and scallop-shell birdbath. Chores are minimal: an occasional raking of the paths, spading between rows to keep the plants from spreading, some shearing, a cocoa-hull mulch in spring, a late-fall salt-hay or pine-bough comforter to keep roots securely in place through New England winter freezes and thaws.

*THE PLAN*
1. *Japanese holly* (Ilex crenata stokesii)
2. *Chives* (Allium schoenoprasum) *with lavender-pink bloom, and runnerless alpine strawberries* (Fragaria Baron von Solemacher), *with white flowers*
3. *Roman wormwood* (Artemisia pontica) *with silvery foliage*
4. *Green santolina* (S. virens) *with yellow bloom*
5. *Lemon thyme* (Thymus serpyllum aureum) *with yellow-margined leaves*
6. *Sweet marjoram* (Majorana hortensis), *with whitish flowers, a tender perennial grown as an annual*
7. *Sage* (Salvia officinalis), *gray leaves, blue blossoms*
8. *Thrift, Sea Pink* (Armeria maritima lauchenana), *pink*
9. *Cheddar Pink* (Dianthus gratianopolitanus, D. caesius), *with white-pink blossoms*
10. *Houseleek, hen-and-chickens* (Sempervivum tectorum) *in strawberry jar*

**4** Vegetables and herbs can be as pretty as flowers—in fact, some are flowers—yet too often gardeners tuck them off in the back-forty or fail to grow them unless they have a lot of room. If space is limited, imagination and palate need not be. Robert Ackart's front yard is colorful with tiny tomatoes, Ruby lettuce rosettes, white blossoming garden rocket, lavender-pink blossoming chives. And weekend planting, harvesting, and weeding are easily done in minutes.

## A vest-pocket salad garden by a front door

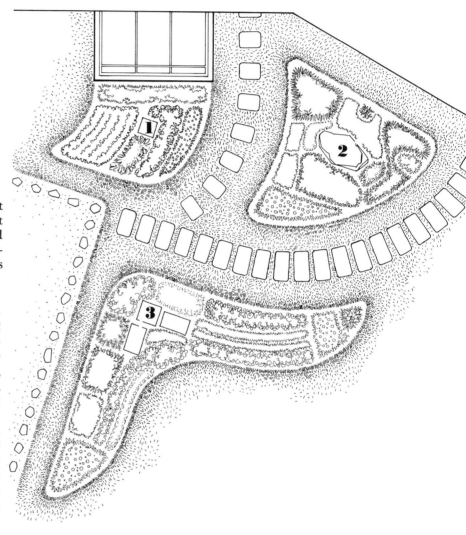

In this ideally level, sunny spot between driveway and front door, good things from seed flourish all summer, and perennial herbs survive the rigors of New York winters.

*THE PLAN*

1. *Garden near a tiny greenhouse measures 9 feet and contains Italian flat and curly parsley, five kinds of lettuce (Ruby, Buttercrunch, Bibb, Slowbolt, Salad Bowl), dill, radishes, and garden rocket (Eruca sativa).*

2. *Triangular garden around a boulder near the house has perennial chives (common fine leaf, garlic broad leaf), rosemary, tarragon, oregano, thyme (lemon, silver, ornamental red, white, woolly), santolina, and strawberries.*

3. *Long, curving garden about 19 feet from tip to tip, golden with marigolds, has lettuce, bushy green and Dark Opal basil, Patio tomatoes, lemon balm, sage, summer savory, sweet marjoram, garden rocket. Biweekly sowings of lettuce and garden rocket keep these greens coming until frost. Basil makes new leaves all season if pinched on top, not allowed to flower.*

The Thrifty Cookbook *by Mr. Ackart has some of his herb recipes. Tip for easier gardening: A few stepping-stones inside each bed permits harvesting after rain.*

## An organic vegetable patch by a swimming pool

Student Kirk Beckwith wanted to try organic gardening—no chemical fertilizers, no sprays, but plenty of grass clippings as mulch, and companion plants to fight pests. His space was limited to a sunny strip between swimming pool and evergreens. His time was short: a summer vacation at home from Reed College in Oregon. The season was short, too. Home is cool Connecticut, and he could not plant until early June. His harvest for the family table outdid his hopes.

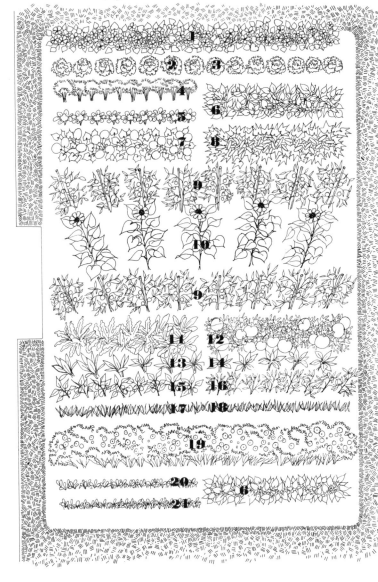

After spading the 20-foot garden, Kirk Beckwith mixed dried manure, sludge, and other organic nutrients into the soil and seeded short rows of annual vegetables and flowers. Slow-growing tomatoes, eggplant, peppers, and a few herbs were nursery seedlings. Onions were grown from sets (bulbs). He put in protective hedges of marigolds and nasturtiums that repel nematodes and aphids. A mulch between rows kept moisture in and weeds out. When borers threatened the zucchini and pumpkins, he dusted the stems with wood ashes and had no further trouble.

*THE PLAN*

| | |
|---|---|
| *1. Nasturtiums* | *12. Bush pumpkins* |
| *2. Lettuce* | *13. Swiss chard* |
| *3. Spinach* | *14. Beets* |
| *4. Herbs* | *15. Eggplant* |
| *5. Broccoli* | *16. Peppers* |
| *6. Beans* | *17. Onions* |
| *7. Cantaloupe* | *18. Chives* |
| *8. Cucumbers* | *19. Marigolds* |
| *9. Tomatoes* | *20. Radishes* |
| *10. Sunflower* | *21. Carrots* |
| *11. Zucchini* | |

# 6

From his front porch and from a wood and stone tower, topped by a gleaming deer and garlanded by wild grapes, Albert Keidel can survey his garden set in the Texas hill country. The hills in spring wear an Indian blanket of wildflowers, but most of the time the land is tawny, except for the small lawn, evergreen live oaks, and his undaunted hardy plants.

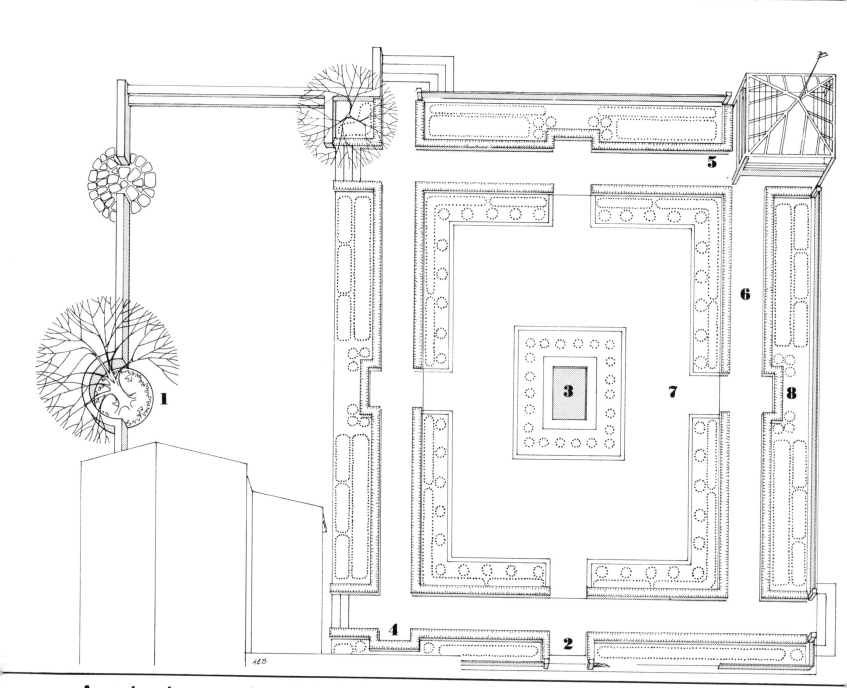

**An enclosed green garden with hardy plants and a tower for looking out**

Albert Keidel's front yard began as a few live oaks clustered near a pioneer log cabin, which had acquired a low stone wing in the 1890s. Green shade now dapples an enlarged two-story ranch house. A stone wall, curved to preserve a scrawny oak (now a nurtured giant), frames a terrace for entertaining. The 53-by-61-foot enclosure with a tower gazebo can be maintained with limited water, minimal care. Lawns in the Southwest have to be watered often, so Mr. Keidel grows a heat-resistant grass confined to a minimum area. Along with hardy plants, much of the garden's strength lies in Albert Keidel's ingenious use of native timber and stone.

## THE PLAN

*1. An evergreen live oak and, 2., an existing gateway fixed the position of 3., the small pool. 4. A bedroom window by a front walk suggested a path parallel to the terrace and an exit near a crape myrtle tree. After that, 5. and 6., the other paths and a tower fell neatly into place. The paths are river-pebble mosaics lined with dwarf boxwood. 7. A small lawn of St. Augustine grass around the pool is framed by day lilies and 12-inch spheres of dwarf yaupon, a southern holly. 8. Niches in each outer bed are flanked by columnar variegated euonymus for height. The euonymus is 3 feet now, will attain 5 or 6 feet.*

## THE PLANTS

*In this climate, and with the help of water piped from a spring to a nearby tank, some vines and flowers keep their green leaves much of the year, and the blossoms provide seasonal color. Wisteria drapes the terrace wall. A vigorous Lady Banksia yellow rose covers the porch overhang. Leaves of this Old South rose are virtually evergreen. Around the pool are hardy windflowers (the bulb, Anemone blanda) in spring, then portulaca for hot, dry summers. The shallow pool holds a transplanted native water lily and cattail. The outer borders are stippled in summer with yellow and orange day lilies and trumpet vine, white shasta daisies, and perennial white phlox. Pot plants—amaryllis, oleander, clivia, geraniums—bloom on the Mexican tile porch and terrace. (Their winter home is a no-trouble greenhouse, a sheep shed protected by corrugated plastic sides.)*

A finely detailed fence and all but the stone corner of the 20-foot-tall, 8½-foot-square tower, built like a partially framed house, were made of cypress timbers from the hill country, salvaged from an abandoned railroad's water tank. Sold for scrap, the wood was cut to Mr. Keidel's design, stained, and antiqued with enough whitewash to cling to the grain. The railroad had linked San Antonio and Fredericksburg, a town his great-grandfather helped settle and where Mr. Keidel, an architect, has restored early houses. For his own log cabin he added a wood second story and balcony. He doubled the old limestone wing by tearing down one end to have enough stone to build a second-floor studio. Having no more stone cut by the original German craftsmen, and being firmly opposed to mismatching, he filled the end with a glass gable upstairs and a glass door below, which now opens to the garden. The terrace wall was made of natural flat stone mellowed with copper sulfate to blend in with the cut stone of the house itself.

*THE PATHS of this garden were inspired by Old World craftsmen, yet can be copied as a family project even children can share. The 4-foot paths were framed by wood and filled with 3 inches of sand and gravel. Next, flagstones with straight edges were placed along the sides. A dry mixture of sand and cement was spread between the stone borders, and then the design: a mosaic of dry, smooth river rocks and pebbles, arranged and dusted as needed until everyone was pleased with the pattern. A board was pressed down to firm the mosaic, and water lightly sprinkled with a 10-inch brush or old broom dipped in a pail—just enough to set the cement. Five feet is enough to do at a time and, like a green garden, the beauty lasts.*

"In a small space everything must count," photographer Ernst Beadle says. "Foliage must be interesting and flowers long-blooming." Shelves, arbors, fences, and walls are his acreage in a leafy terrace 9 feet at its widest. He thinks heavy topsoil is outdated for container gardening, and he uses soilless mixes to lighten stress on roof beams and back. He rigged up an automatic watering system to keep the garden going in his absence. He also has a trouble-free fish pond. Roses, he finds, love city life and thrive on city air.

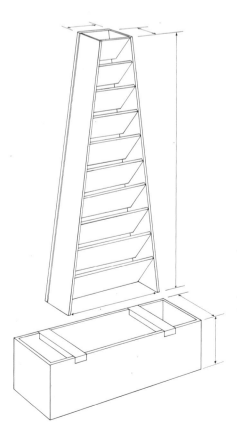

*OBELISK for rock plants is made of redwood, with a backing of waterproof plywood. Each shelf is canted and flush with the front but stops short of the ¾-inch plywood by 2 inches. This provides pockets for planting and a vertical wall of potting soil at the back. A daily trickle of water from a concealed hose at the top keeps the vertical soil layer moist. A plastic sheet between plywood and brick wall prevents any seepage. Mr. Beadle filled the obelisk with sharp-drainage perlite mixed with humus and agricultural lime. The obelisk is 1 foot wide at the top; the bottom is 3 feet wide; the sides are 8-by-1-foot planks. The obelisk rests on two-by-fours on a box 5 feet long, 18 inches deep and wide.*

*VINES: Boston ivy, akebia (A. quinata), Madeira vine, Concord grape, morning glory, espaliered pyracantha*
*TREES: Golden willow (Salix alba tristis), weeping crabapple (Malus, Red Jade)*
*FOLIAGE PLANTS: Caladium tubers planted in spring, lifted in fall, fancy-leaf geraniums, scented geraniums, artemisias, hosta, Spanish bayonet, pampas and fountain grasses, rue, centaurea, culinary herbs*
*FLOWERS: Roses (tree, bush, and miniatures for three levels of bloom), Queen Elizabeth, Apricot Nectar, Angel Face, Tiffany, others. Tropical water lily, marigolds, portulaca, nicotiana, chrysanthemums, hundreds of grape hyacinth (Muscari armeniacum) and Darwin Hybrid Emperor tulips*
*VEGETABLES: Tomatoes, cucumbers, lettuce, Chinese melons*
*HOUSE PLANTS: Ficus benjamina, palms, pittosporum, grape ivy, ferns, calamondin orange*

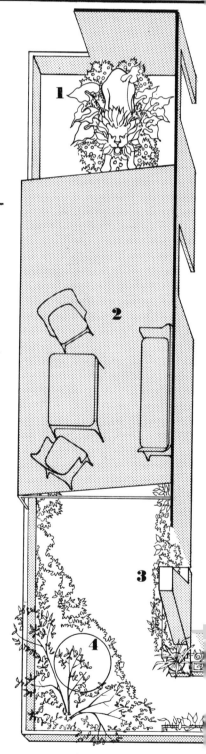

*VINES* are quick and easy, Mr. Beadle says. "You need them in a city garden, and you need them for comfort—otherwise the walls absorb heat and reflect it back—and for screening. They also give an illusion of distance and depth. You know there is something behind the leaves, but it no longer seems just a blank wall." At his place, screening out a water tank was important, so he has a morning-glory arbor, "extra fancy, aggressively *there,* so you would have to notice it and not the tank." Mr. Beadle uses only deciduous vines that produce fresh leaves each spring. Except for Boston ivy that clings to bricks, his vines twist on green vinyl-covered wire fencing, a 3-inch mesh nailed to walls and arbors.

*PLANTING BOXES* for outdoor use in a cold area should be at least 18 inches deep and 18 inches wide. Frost penetrates 2 to 6 inches from all directions, so 18 inches can keep the center unfrozen and the plants alive. A wood planter must have drainage holes on the sides or bottom and should be set on feet or blocks to allow for drainage and air circulation. Most of Mr. Beadle's containers are made of redwood, which he allows to weather and turn gray like the stone and cement sculpture, "found art," he spots and buys at demolition sites. *Sedum acre,* planted in each box, has slip-covered the boxes with leaves.

*WATERING* should be done individually, he believes, but he often has to be away, photographing other people's houses and gardens, so an automatic timer from a greenhouse company sees to it that the garden gets watered anyway. Mr. Beadle ran a hose over the tops of containers, obelisk, and arbors and simply made seepage holes with a $\frac{1}{16}$th-inch electric drill.

*LIGHTWEIGHT POTTING MIXES* are all Mr. Beadle uses, except for a few top-heavy plants like his orange tree. "You'd think plants would turn up their noses at synthetic soil, but they love it." These so-called peat-lite or Cornell mixes are easy to handle and are sold in garden centers under various trade names. A Cornell formula you can mix on your own calls for: ½ bushel each of vermiculite and shredded peat moss; 4 tablespoons powdered limestone; 1 tablespoon superphosphate-20; 8 to 16 teaspoons of all-purpose 5-10-5 fertilizer. Mr. Beadle also adds slow-release organic fertilizer in spring and midsummer, "and dried cow manure as soon as I can close the windows in fall."

*AIR,* like water and soil, is a special consideration in city gardening. "Some plants, like the rose family, take to polluted urban air, and some do not. An important thing to know about New York City gardening is that the air is acid." Mr. Beadle offsets this by adding lime every year to most containers.

*A TROUBLE-FREE FISH POND* is easy to make, with the use of an asbestos-cement planter. With a cork placed firmly in the drainage hole, Mr. Beadle's pond glints all summer with goldfish and water lilies. The fish get along on insects and are given away in fall. The cork is then pulled, and the water goes down the building's drain.

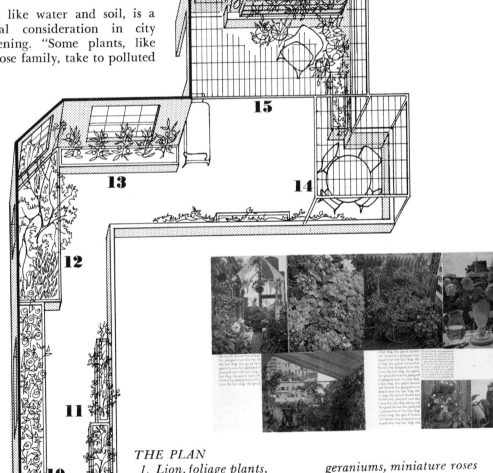

THE PLAN
1. Lion, foliage plants, flowers
2. Seating area with awning
3. Obelisk for rock plants
4. Fish pond and willow
5. Roses
6. Ivy and caladiums
7. Morning-glory arch
8. Fern rack for scented geraniums, miniature roses
9. Weeping crabapple
10. Roses
11. Pyracantha
12. Herbs
13. Tomatoes
14. Vine-shaded area
15. Wall shelves for grape hyacinths, caladiums

101

**A dooryard of fragrant herbs and a walk-through herb garden in a meadow**

8 Jack and Esther Larson use herbs to accent good food, to hang in closets, and to make fresh and dried bouquets. Mrs. Larson, a painter and fashion illustrator, loves their garden also for its "simplicity, so right for this kind of house; for the colors, the restful grays, greens, and blue-greens; and for the cheerfulness of the blossoms all spring and summer." The Larsons find that very little has to be planted from year to year, except for annuals like basil and sweet alyssum, but occasionally their Connecticut neighbor, Adelma G. Simmons, comes over from her Caprilands Herb Farm with new plants. Herbs are not as thirsty, hungry, or disease prone as many other plants. Dryish, well-drained soil, somewhat light and granular, helps them remember those Mediterranean hillsides from which so many came. A neutral to alkaline pH is ideal for most. Where soil is acid, a little pulverized agricultural lime or some wood ashes or crushed eggshells will help. The two herbs the Larsons keep in pots are sweet bay, a perennial tree with glossy leaves, and rosemary, a short-needled evergreen. Both need more frequent watering than most other herbs, and both make handsome house plants that can be snipped for cooking all winter.

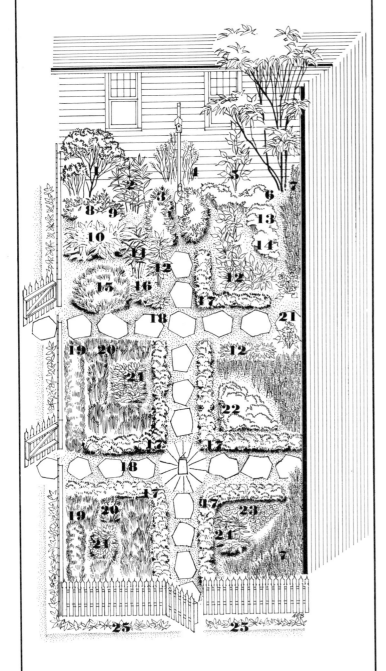

**1**
*Sweet bay*
(Laurus nobilis)

**2**
*Lemon verbena*
(Lippia citriodora)

**3**
*Parsley*
(Petroselinum crispum,
P. latifolium)

**4**
*Lovage*
(Levisticum officinale)

**5**
*Angelica*
(Archangelica officinalis)

**6**
*Sweet woodruff*
(Asperula odorata)

**7**
*Rosemary*
(Rosmarinus officinalis)

**8**
*Mints*
(Mentha piperita,
M. rotundifolia, others)

**9**
*Chives*
(Allium schoenoprasum)

**10**
*Catnip*
(Nepeta cataria)

**11**
*Basil*
(Ocimum basilicum,
Dark Opal)

**12**
*Strawberries*
(Fragaria vesca)

**13**
*Sweet marjoram*
(Majorana hortensis)

**14**
*Sweet Cicely*
(Myrrhis odorata)

**15**
*Sage*
(Salvia officinalis)

**16**
*Winter savory*
(Satureia montana)

**17**
*Sweet alyssum*
(Lobularia maritima)

**18**
*Thyme*
(Thymus vulgaris)

**19**
*Germander*
(Teucrium chamaedrys)

**20**
*Lavender*
(Lavandula officinalis)

**21**
*Violets and
Johnny-jump-ups*
(Violas)

**22**
*Southernwood*
(Artemisia abrotanum)

**23**
*Candytuft*
(Iberis sempervirens)

**24**
*Lemon balm*
(Melissa officinalis)

**25**
*Climbing strawberries*
(Fragaria, var.)

*This is a kitchen garden,
sweet-smelling to sit by
(especially in the rain)
or just to walk past on the
way to the front door.
It measures 12 by 22 feet,
is enclosed by a weathered
picket fence.*

**A dooryard of fragrant herbs and a walk-through herb garden in a meadow**

8 Herb gardens are ideal for busy people. The Larsons' dooryard of culinary herbs, with a few ornamental exceptions, proved so delightful and undemanding that they were inspired to plan this larger one in a meadow. It is pretty to look at from a garden terrace above it. It is fragrant to walk through and even to walk past to get to the field nearby. It is made up of little gardens, easy to take care of. Chores in an herb garden are not arduous. Vigorous growers, herbs may need to be divided and cut back in fall, but the task is downright pleasurable. If any leaves or stems are accidentally bruised or broken, herbs forgive with delicious fragrance. Harvesting herbs is continuous, slow-paced. At almost any time they can be cut for the kitchen or bouquets, or dried or frozen for winter use. Artemisias can be at their best in autumn; if wired as silvery swags or wreaths, some, like Silver King (*A. albula*), make handsome Christmas decorations. In deep winter, when this garden is covered with snow, "We visit it on snowshoes," Esther Larson says, "even though all you can see is the top of the sundial and pear tree. Snow is the ideal winter mulch." When spring comes, New England's mud time, the Larsons add a mulch of cocoa hulls, "our April fudge," and that keeps weeding simple.

**1**
Fence borders of sweetbrier (eglantine) roses with false indigo (Baptisia), tall artemisias (A. abrotanum, A. albula, A. lactifolia), delphiniums, lilies, tansy (Tanacetum), yarrow (Achillea), rosemary, others

**2**
Decorative bee skep and gate to vegetable garden beyond

**3**
Corner bed of blueberries, old-fashioned shrub roses, scented geraniums, mints, with germander border, and old stone sink providing water for birds

**4**
Old-fashioned shrub roses, spring bulbs, germander border

**5**
Pear tree

**6**
Gray and green santolinas, savory, sage

**7**
Potentilla (P. fruticosa) with yellow blossoms all summer

**8**
Quince tree, yellow day lilies, Silver Mound and other low-growing artemisias (A. schmidtiana nana, A. pontica),

Lady's bedstraw (Galium), lamb's ears (Stachys lanata) border

**9**
Quince, artemisias, rue, Lady's mantle (Alchemilla), lamb's ears

**10**
Gray garden of catnip, dianthus, dusty millers (Artemisia stelleriana and others, Centaurea cineraria and gymnocarpa, senecios)

**11**
Thyme and sundial

**12**
Starwort garden between fence and steppingstones— asters, marguerites, feverfew (Chrysanthemum parthenium), pot marigold (Calendula officinalis); calendula petals sprinkled on salads are said to be "good for the heart, the complexion, and the disposition"

This is a strolling garden with a maze of brick paths zigzagging through herb beds, each one different. Two chairs, two birdbaths, and two beehives are all but hidden.

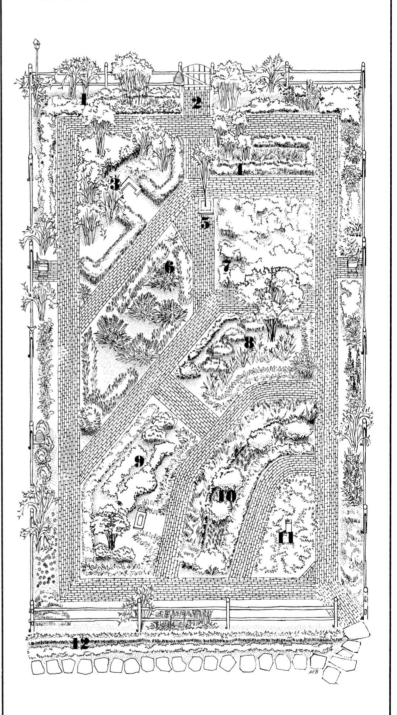

# 9

**A small green garden with a lilac walk**

*THE PLAN*

1. *Yew hedge* (Taxus media hatfieldii)
2. *Flagstone path*
3. *Border of periwinkle, also called myrtle* (Vinca minor) *dotted with a few cotoneasters* (C. dammerii) *and hardy shrubs and trees*
4. *Boule de Neige rhododendron*
5. *Dwarf hinoki cypress* (Chamaecyparis obtusa compacta)
6. *Dwarf Korean lilac standards clipped like parasols* (Syringa palibiniana)
7. *Japanese quince* (Chaenomeles japonica)
8. *Dogwood* (Cornus florida)
9. *Marble-chip path*
10. *Crisscross pattern of dwarf English boxwood* (Buxus sempervirens suffruticosa) *framing and dividing the 10-by-20-foot flower bed. Center bed usually has blue and white pansies in spring, and dusty millers, gray santolina, and deep pink geraniums, plunged in the bed in their pots, from summer to the first frost of autumn*

Because this formal garden was designed for minimal upkeep, Laura Bishop easily keeps it to perfection. "In a little garden, work is pleasant because there is not much of it." Beautiful in all seasons, it has evergreen borders that demand only an annual clipping to stay neat and healthy. Six perky lilac trees and several shrubs that bloom punctually each spring explode the green geometry. The garden offers the serenity of unchanging green and the joy of experimentation. Like a centerpiece on a table, the center bed holds changeable flowers that vary with the seasons.

*The terrace, edged by evergreen pachysandra and rhododendrons, has a small pool and fountain half-wreathed with small-leaved English ivy and summer pots of white petunias. The ivy arc is just one vigorous plant. What Mrs. Bishop longed for was a little garden, "attractive to look at from the terrace." What*

*Eloise A. Ray of Westport, Connecticut, designed is a jewel box of a sunken garden, "someone once said a prayer rug of a garden," to enjoy at any season and even at night. White flowers and paths glimmer at dusk. Two down lights at the tops of dogwood trees illuminate the garden, while two small up lights tucked*

*behind two hinoki cypresses light the gate that leads to a swimming pool. The pool, also designed by Mrs. Ray, has "no hardware," no ladder or diving board, and is "a reflecting pool we swim in." It is edged with thick flagstone and was painted inside with a putty color that turns, under water, to a subtle blue.*

The six lilacs, a dwarf round-headed type, are grown on slim trunks 36 to 40 inches tall. The symmetrical heads are covered in June with lavender-pink flowers. Mrs. Bishop clips the trees after bloom to keep the twigs in a topiary parasol-like form. The garden gate repeats the crisscross pattern of the dividers in the center bed. It is stained brown and brushed every few years with protective boiled linseed oil. Posts of native stone with raked, unmortared joints are starred each June with white Henryi clematis.

*Clipping is the main chore required and enjoyed here. The yew hedge is sheared in summer and kept at 30 inches, narrower at the top than at the bottom. This shape permits sunlight to strike the low branches, which, if shaded, could become thin and scraggly. Boxwood*

*is clipped in summer to hold its spherical form and shielded in winter with yew clippings. They are stuck upright in the ground like a new winter hedge, and the covering is removed in early spring. Vinca is groomed in spring to remove any winterkill. Vinca, incidentally, is fed*

*bonemeal (like the lilacs) though most evergreens take an acid fertilizer. When rhododendrons have bloomed, their seed heads are snapped off to promote plant vigor. This gardener prefers to see the earth in beds and so does not mulch. Impertinent weeds are promptly uprooted.*

# A whispering garden in the Japanese manner enclosed for serenity

**10** When Jean Arthur's friends speak of her garden (she will neither praise nor explain it, only praise those who helped her build this private world), their words conjure up her whispering garden and also the timbre of the actress's unforgettable voice. The sensitive use of scale and color, and interplay of smooth and rough textures, make her garden, like her voice, catch at the heart. It is a shy garden.

Simplicity, Japanese style: In this garden a quiet pool reflects restless treetops, and ancient redwood rounds set in a lawn of delicate babies' tears seem almost to float in a tranquil green sea. Because the garden suits its terrain so perfectly, it belies the discipline that went into its creation. A need for privacy inspired the Japanese-style torii gate and 6-foot redwood wall, now silvery gray from the sea wind. From the gate curving paths lead inward past changing patterns of ground cover. Classic Japanese elements include stone lanterns and the traditional pond garden for strolling and the dry-landscape garden. Most of the design for the outer and inner gardens was by landscape architect George Hoy, and Frank Vanderveen of Carmel, California. Mr. Hoy discovered at a logging site the enormous redwood rounds he brought here to use as occasional stepping-stones and as "little oases to rest the eye, to sit on, to stretch out on in the sun." Designer Brad Bowman was tapped for his expertise in stonework and walkways. In recent years Yoshiko Tanamoto, master teacher of *ikebana,* has renewed the plantings. "What Jean wanted and achieved," said a friend of many years, "was a sanctuary, a quiet place so necessary for tranquillity and well-being."

*THE PLANTS
a partial list:
The ground-hugging house has walls leafy with fatshedera* (F. lizei) *and ivy. The lawn is not grass, or moss as one sees in Japan, but creeping mosslike babies' tears* (Helxine soleirolii)*, often grown in greenhouse pots. It is sometimes edged by a pink-flowering erodium* (E. chamaedryoides)*. Monterey cypresses* (Cupressus macrocarpa)*, a low juniper chinensis near the front door, taller junipers, and a gnarled Japanese black pine* (Pinus thunbergii, *especially good in coastal areas*) *are among the many conifers. Ornamental grasses include tufts of Japanese grass* (Ophiopogan japonicus) *and lily-turf* (Liriope spicata)*. Near the gate are a spiny aloe and red montbretia* (Tritonia)*. Staghorn and other ferns grow in the plant room.*

## A casual riverside garden with her perennials, his rock plants

Peace and quiet, American-style, can be a plashing river, a natural garden, and the soothing reminder that "the accidental flower gives a garden charm." Weekend gardeners Dr. and Mrs. Louis Wardell "try to assist nature or leave things undisturbed." They assist by fertilizing nature's sowings and occasionally pruning woodland growth too exuberant for its own good. Dr. Wardell has a garden of self-reliant plants chinked in a wall. Mrs. Wardell cultivates perennials not fussy about wet feet.

T

The only really dry spot at the Wardells' is the wall by the gravel driveway. It is made of stones excavated when they enlarged and winterized their weekend house. Made without mortar, the wall has the gravelly earth pockets and good drainage that rock gardens require. From the driveway a pathway of old millstones leads to the terrace. A river millstone set on a stump became a picnic table in the nearby grape arbor. The fieldstone terrace is near a onetime screened porch, now a glassed-in room full of river-reflected light for pot plants. Here the Wardells can watch turtles sun on the opposite bank, and birds feed their young. At twilight kerosene torches are reflected in the river. The torches are easily slipped into vertical pipes mortared to the edge of the terrace. Clay pots of geraniums serve as a balustrade. Beyond the porch, Mrs. Wardell has planted a hill cascade of perennials that prefer or do not mind dampness. She fights nature only on the matter of white phlox and roses, which she loves too much to forgo. "Phlox gets mildew, roses get blackspot, and so I have to spray to have them." Otherwise, the Wardells see things nature's way.

### ROCK PLANTS

Aubrietia (A. aubrietia, magenta-purple flowers)
Basket-of-gold (Alyssum saxatile, yellow)
Bellflower (Campanula carpatica, C. rotundifolia, blue)
Candytuft (Iberis sempervivum, white)
Coralbells (Heuchera sanguinea, light red)
Cranesbill (Geranium lancastriense, pink)
Dianthus (Maiden Pink, D. deltoides; Cheddar Pink, D. gratianopolitanus and caesius)
Houseleek, Hen-and-chickens (Sempervivum tectorum, succulent with fleshy leaves)
Iceland poppy (Papaver nudicaule, yellow)

Phlox (Moss Pink, P. subulata; P. divaricata, lavender)
Potentilla (P. alpestris, P. fruticosa, yellow)
Rock cress (Arabis, white)
Snow-in-summer (Cerastium tomentosum, white)
Stonecrop (Sedum sieboldii, pink; S. acre, yellow)
Thrift, Sea Pink (Armeria maritima, pink)
Thyme (Thymus serpyllum, pink-purple)
Veronica (V. repens, V. serpyllifolia, blue)

### WEEKEND GARDENERS

should forgo big lawns requiring mowing and upkeep, "if they have a choice," Mrs. Wardell says. The Wardells use ground covers such as blue-flowered vinca, pachysandra, and English ivy, all of which stay green all year. "Sedums and succulents also make a wonderful cover on rock ledges and require no upkeep at all." They also recommend shrubs that bloom at different times—forsythia, quince, lilacs, rhododendrons, weigela, rose of Sharon (Hibiscus syriacus). Maintenance is a matter of occasional pruning and fertilization. The Wardells save fireplace ashes for lilacs, "and, since we started composting, things really pop."

**A kitchen yard of herbs growing in wooden boxes** transformed the stony 13-by-20-foot area just outside the Frank MacGregor Smiths' back door. It had been their problem area where grass grew poorly and an uninteresting privet hedge separated them from a neighbor. It was, in fact, "fit only for the clothesline." The framework of the garden makes it comforting to look at even in winter, and by late spring fresh herbs can be gathered conveniently for the salad bowl or casserole, or to give as a nosegay to a visitor.

## THE PLAN
1. *Privet hedge*
2. *English ivy and lamb's ears* (Stachys lanata)
3. *Shade-loving sweet woodruff* (Asperula odorata)
4. *Narrow boxes filled with southernwood artemisia* (A. abrotanum) *and green santolina* (S. virens) *around paths*
5. *A center bed with wood dividers for such decorative herbs as lavender, rue, Johnny-jump-up, and pot marigold*
6. *Bed with a sundial on a stump*
7. *Culinary herbs such as parsley, sage, rosemary, thyme (common, lemon, English, and French), chives and other alliums, winter savory, tarragon, sweet marjoram, basil, and others. These herbs winter over under salt hay, except for basil, and for tender rosemary, which is potted and brought inside*
8. *Silver Mound artemisia* (A. schmidtiana nana), *sage, and lamb's ears near steppingstones*
9. *Spearmint and applemint that are planted near the kitchen door*

Collecting for the house can include collecting plants appropriate to its period and place. The simple herb garden behind the Smiths' pre-Revolutionary house in Westchester County, New York, was discovered, appropriately but unexpectedly, as a living display at an antiques show. Its fence and boxes are made of weathered boards. To replace any of the wood as needed, the Smiths collect random boards and leave them outdoors to turn a suitable, venerable gray. Most of the herbs carry over from year to year, but Adelma G. Simmons, who designed the garden, helps the Smiths refurbish it from time to time by sending seeds and plants from her Caprilands Herb Farm in Coventry, Connecticut.

## A LITTLE GARDEN OF CULINARY HERBS TO GROW IN BOXES OR POTS

*All of these herbs can be grown indoors near a sunny window or under fluorescent light:*

BASIL (Ocimum basilicum), *broad-leaved, bushy annual, grows 1 to 2 feet*
BAY (Laurus nobilis), *perennial tree with glossy leaves, 4 to 10 feet*
CHERVIL (Anthriscus cerefolium), *parsleylike annual, 1 to 2 feet*
CHIVES (Allium schoenoprasum), *perennial, grasslike clumps, 6 inches to 1 foot*
CORIANDER (Coriandrum sativum), *annual with delicate leaves, 1 to 2 feet*
DILL (Anethum graveolens), *tall annual with feathery leaves, 2 to 3 feet*
LEMON BALM (Melissa officinalis), *perennial, crinkly leaves, 1 to 2 feet*
LEMON VERBENA (Lippia citriodora), *tender shrubby perennial, 1 to 10 feet*
MINT (Mentha piperita, *others*), *crinkly perennial, 1 to 3 feet*
OREGANO (Origanum vulgaris, *a form of sweet marjoram*), *6 inches to 1 foot*
PARSLEY (Petroselinum crispum), *curly, cut-leaf biennial, 1 to 1½ feet*
ROSEMARY (Rosmarinus officinalis), *tender, perennial evergreen, 3 to 5 feet*
SAGE (Salvia officinalis), *gray-green perennial, 1 to 2 feet*
SAVORY (Satureia montana—*winter*), *woody perennial, 2 feet*
SWEET MARJORAM (Majorana hortensis), *perennial, 6 inches to 1 foot*
TARRAGON (Artemisia dracunculus), *slim, twisting perennial, 2 feet*
THYME (Thymus vulgaris, *others*), *tiny-leaved perennial, 6 inches to 1 foot*

Ken Scott, a Midwesterner transplanted to Milan, has a garden on top of a building—a lush jungle of pot plants, and a pavilion and deck painted green. Originally, he had just a tarred roof, a rim around a glass-brick roof one story down, which he treated as a plant-filled atrium. This is the restful oasis this designer needs, yet it is "all temporary. As a renter I could remove it if I had to."

**A green garden on a city rooftop where everything grows in pots**

# 13

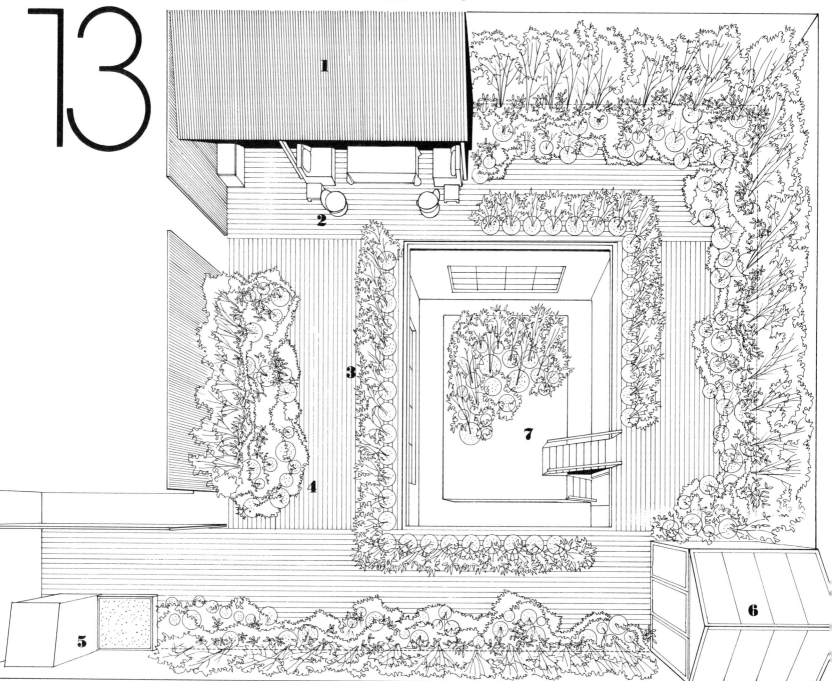

To have some shade for daytime dining, Mr. Scott had a lightweight metal pavilion built and bolted to the decking. It, too, can be taken apart if needed. Its canopy is translucent corrugated plastic, camouflaged by sandwiching the plastic between layers of reed matting. Reed is also used on some vertical surfaces. Mint-green banquettes and cushions enclose three sides of a dining table. Green curtains on drawstrings give protection on chilly nights. Mr. Scott bought a small prefab greenhouse as a place to winter his oleanders, to care for ailing plants, and "to get a month's jump on spring by starting plants from seed."

THE PLAN
1. Dining pavilion
2. Decking
3. Balustrade of tree roses
4. Vines and other plants
5. Storage area for soil
6. Prefab greenhouse
7. Atrium garden on glass-brick roof of showroom

THE PLANTS
a partial listing:
VINES
English ivy and deciduous vines in pots are set permanently along the wall. In summer Heavenly Blue morning glories (Ipomea) and cup-and-saucers (Cobaea scandens) clamber up strings and mingle with the ivy.
FOLIAGE PLANTS
Bamboo, willow, and house plants out in season—rubber plant, dracaena, schefflera, Boston fern, others.
FLOWERS
Tree roses, flowering house plants in season—oleanders, begonias, fuchsias, and flowers started from seed, such as

dahlias (tubers are saved and replanted each spring), wallflowers, marigolds, cosmos, zinnias, four-o'clocks, nicotiana. "Working people ought to have flowers that are at their best in early morning, like morning glories, or in late afternoon and evening, like four-o'clocks and fragrant white nicotiana."

Everything here grows in terra-cotta pots instead of treated wood boxes or metal containers favored by some city gardeners. Mr. Scott uses terra-cotta pots because "they are cheap in Italy, and I don't have to worry about their cracking because our winters are not severe." He compares the climate in Milan with that of Washington, D.C., and other cities farther south. Summers are hot, snow flies occasionally, but freezes are not deep. Roses, however, are winter-mulched with straw. He repots the roses every two years but finds "most plants can live for decades in a clay pot as long as they have healthy amounts of water and fertilizer." Any container garden requires frequent watering because of the limited soil depth. A city rooftop has the additional hazard of drying winds. His plants are watered individually with a hose each day, and both morning and evening on hottest days. "Frequent waterings take nutrients out fast," so plants are fertilized once in February, March, and April, and after that every two weeks till fall. Mr. Scott uses commercial fertilizers in dry and liquid forms. His planting medium is earth mixed with peat moss. To maintain a steady supply of flowers, he starts seeds in peat pots in the greenhouse every three weeks in spring and early summer. Seedlings are transplanted, peat pot and all, to terra-cotta pots. In fall the soil in pots where annuals grew is dumped in a storage pile, fertilized, and left, to be used again the following spring.

On the tarred roof above his apartment and showroom, Mr. Scott put down decking to provide a cool surface for plants and for walking, and to distribute weight, an important consideration in planning a roof garden. The planks are painted pale green and set on a wood grid of two-by-fours that permits air to circulate and thus evaporate spills from watering and prevent the deck from rotting. "A wood deck is less heavy than tile, less expensive, long-lasting, and easily removable."

For Mrs. Hugh O. Hencken (botanical name: Thalassa Cruso), the Cape Cod summer place where the family gathers is also an idea workshop for her garden books and television shows. A former vegetable garden became a formal cutting garden. On a shady porch house plants get "rest and recreation to recover from their winter woes."

## A well-designed cutting garden and a porch garden of house plants

Visitors to this turn-of-the-century summer place are greeted by Thalassa Cruso's porch garden. Her "rex begonias that multiplied into a whole dynasty" occupy a triangular stand built to fit a corner. Easygoing succulents grow on planks that hang on the wall. Flowers in pots are staged on steps in a lighted alcove. Thalassa Cruso believes in "staging," setting plants at different levels outdoors and indoors. "Stage them on steps," she advises, "or on upturned pots, or on boards set on cinder blocks like bleacher seats. Staging gives each plant elbowroom, shows them all off or hides deficiencies, and makes watering easier." Even her cutting garden is staged with low plants in front and taller plants behind. She also advises, "Learn on house plants and you can garden anywhere. Start with an inexpensive pot plant, so it will not be a disaster if it dies while you're learning on it. Some supermarkets and dime stores have very worthwhile plants.

*Talk to plants? "A plant you like you hover over. You say, 'Is it looking any better today?' and 'Is that a new leaf?' and 'Good heavens, I hope that's not mealybug!' When you do that, of course, you're breathing carbon dioxide over it, and carbon dioxide is now piped into greenhouses to make things grow."*

Anything that has survived in such a place is tough. There is also nothing wrong with most commercial potting soil, except that for a mature plant it is like baby food. I mix soil with coarse wet peat moss, sand if I can get it, though perlite is a good sand substitute.

"You can tell when to water only by looking at the soil and feeling it. The difficulty is educating people to realize that plants do not wish to be drowned. Sometimes they have to swim for it! If a plant is in a plastic pot it will need only about half as much water as in a porous clay pot. If you have hanging pots, they may need water more often because of rising hot air. If you don't like water dripping down your sleeve, put ice cubes in the hanging pot. It works like a charm. People who travel a great deal ought to grow what I call the neglectables. Succulents—echeveria, kalanchoe, sempervivum.

"There are two things people don't understand about moving plants outdoors for the summer. Far too many think you mean take them out of their pots—once out, they'll never cram back in again. The other thing to consider is how sensitive plants are to sunlight. Even if they have been in a sunny window, put them first in deep shade, dappled shade eventually. If you can't move plants outdoors in summer, group them away from hot sunny windows.

"Plants set outdoors need shade, even the sun lovers. Plants indoors need light, even the shade lovers. Artificial light is one answer. Fluorescent light units are so easy and cost about what one big philodendron costs. I use spots, too, all over the lot, because I can't bear tube lighting by night. But I use fluorescents by day and use them to raise all my seeds for the garden." Her flowers staged in the porch alcove—hydrangeas, achimenes, begonias, plumbago, geraniums, and more—stay in bloom with the help of a three-tube fluorescent light unit rigged up with a timer—on at 6 A.M., off at 6 P.M. They are spotlighted at night.

"I am not entirely an organic gardener. I do use some chemical controls on my trees. But I very much disapprove of using a spray in the house. It can make you feel ill. And in general I agree with organic gardeners that really healthy plants don't get pests. If an infected plant won't respond to a simple home remedy, like a hard spray of cold water, throw it out. Don't be ashamed if a plant dies—nobody succeeds with everything. Composting is an old and good idea, and the organic gardeners who are trying to grow their poison-free vegetables do manage to live off amazingly small plots of land. Put good stuff back into the soil, and it can support unending beautiful plants."

# 14

*The cutting garden, sunny and inviting to birds and to guests, has a rectilinear design gentled by curves and circles. Shade is used to advantage on the porch for many house plants, while sun-loving echeverias are grown in moss on portable planks and look like living collage.*

*To make a plank garden: Staple small-mesh chicken wire to ends and one side of a plank to form an open envelope. Before stuffing it with long-grained sphagnum moss, soak the moss in hot water and let it cool (wear rubber gloves to retrieve it). Put a moss layer on the mesh flap, but make a mixture of half moss and half perlite for drainage to put on the plank side. Join the layers by drawing the mesh over the open side of the plank, then staple. Force holes in stuffing to insert roots. Succulents are ideal for planks, but petunias, marigolds, and some other plants will also thrive. Hook the plank onto a sunny wall. Move the plank to a sunny spot indoors before frost. Always lay the plank flat to water and feed it evenly. Succulents need very little water and very dilute feedings.*

*THE PLAN*
*of cutting garden:*
1. *Old privet hedge defining garden area*
2. *New stone paths to keep garden to manageable size and inviting to strollers*
3. *Grass borders*
4. *Lath pergola with seating area for parties or for viewing the flowers staged in a crescendo of height and color*
5. *Low birdbath, border of blue and white petunias, and beds of lamb's ears, lavender, and dwarf dahlias*
6. *Curved beds of blue Marie Ballard asters, mixed zinnias, blue platycodon and veronica, purple liatris, snapdragons, marigolds, yellow marguerites, gaillardias*
7. *Tall white phlox, asters, and russet heleniums*
8. *Statue at end of path*
9. *Evergreen arc of yew*
10. *Chamaecyparis grown from a cutting, as was the yew*
11. *Goldenrain-trees (Koelreuteria paniculata) set in twin stone circles*
12. *Simple wood gateway in harmony with pergola*

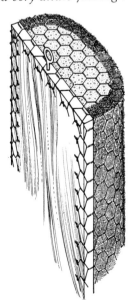

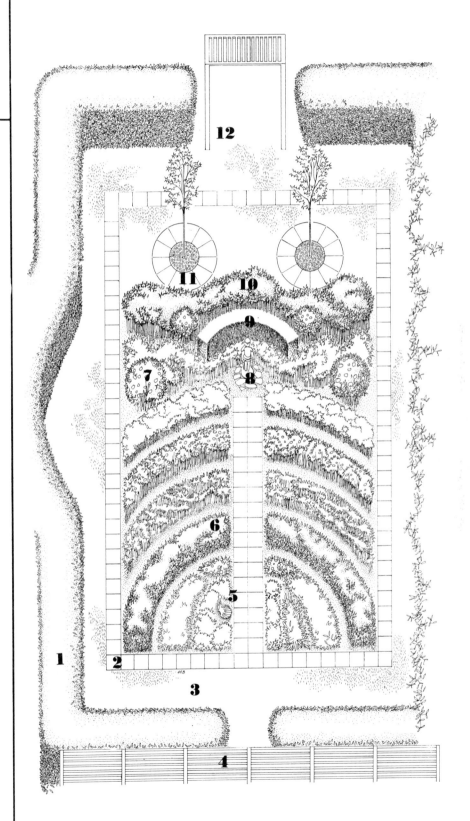

115

# 15

## A canopy of cherry trees and a paisley flower garden

Loops, arcs, and canopies of color enhance the informal country garden of Mr. and Mrs. Thomas B. Hess. Cherry-tree trunks are the columns, and cherry foliage and flowers are the vaulted ceiling of a 10-by-30-foot outdoor dining area. A rose-covered fence, like a lariat around an old corral, frames the three-season cutting garden. A canopy of pines and maples supplies dappled shade for house plants and hanging baskets out on summer holiday.

The Hesses' arbor of pleached cherry trees was made by planting six trees in two rows, with trees spaced 10 feet apart in each direction. The trees are a double pink-flowered form of Japanese flowering cherry, grafted on seven-foot-high trunks of ordinary upright cherry. Their branches are tied at the center. For their first two years the trees were supported by an iron-pipe framework to prevent their leaning toward each other as they grew. Branches that naturally tended to grow upright were bent over and tied toward the center to form the canopy; those that tried to grow outward were cut short to make the outer edge of the canopy denser. Once the structure of pleached branches was established through pruning and interweaving, it was stiff enough to be self-supporting, and the pipe framework was removed. Some of the branches still need to be kept tied. This is done with green garden twine and checked and retied periodically to allow for growth, while wayward branches are pruned each winter to keep the canopy floriferous as well as shapely. Landscape designer: James Fanning.

*The flower garden has a pleasing paisleylike pattern as brick paths loop and arc through multicolor beds neatly mulched with pine bark.*
*IN SPRING*
*Red tulips: Flying Dutchman, Pride of Haarlem, William Pitt, Queen of Sheba*
*Gold tulips: Golden Apeldoorn, Gudoshnik*
*Yellow tulips: Niphetos, Mrs. John T. Scheepers*
*White tulips: Kansas, Sorbet, White Giant, Monsieur S. Mottet*
*Violet-purple tulips: Queen of Night, The Bishop, Demeter, Insurpassable*
*Pink tulips: Renown, China Pink, Her Grace*
*IN SUMMER*
*Clematis: white Henryi, mauve Nelly Moser, Montana rubens*
*Lilies: Madonna, Fiesta hybrids, Lilium auratum, L. speciosum*
*Climbing roses: Blaze, Sea Foam*
*Roses: apricot Mrs. Pierre S. DuPont and Helen Traubel, red Chrysler Imperial,*

*pink Vogue and Queen Elizabeth, yellow Eclipse, others*
*Perennials: Japanese anemones, coralbells*
*Geraniums from pots*
*Summer flowering bulbs: dahlias, tuberoses, acidanthera*
*Annuals for sun: snapdragons, zinnias, marigolds, China asters, gazanias*
*Annuals for shade: impatiens, semperflorens, wax begonias*
*IN FALL*
*Chrysanthemums of many types and shades.*
*POT PLANTS—fuchsias and begonias—are put under shady trees in summer. Some swing in baskets from a pole propped in the crotch of one pine and wire-hung from a taller one. Some are clustered on planks set on cinder blocks.*

A colorful garden is as refreshing in the green Connecticut countryside where the Hesses live as a green garden is in a vibrant city. Here the blast begins in May when tulips fill the cutting garden and flowering cherries just begin to yield to lilacs. Tulips are a center of attention even in peony beds when peony buds are just developing. As tulips drop their petals and their foliage ripens, they are concealed by unfolding peonies. In other beds, when tulips have done their stint, they are lifted and replaced by a crowd of summer annuals, some from pots that have been waiting in cold frames, others seeded where they grow. A tip on seeding: Never cover fine seeds, lightly cover larger seeds, keep moist for good germination. Dahlias and other summer-flowering bulbs, planted in May and lifted in fall, are also clustered among the annuals. Roses, which begin to bloom in June, go on to late fall with no more than a tapering off in the hottest days of midsummer. Meanwhile, in part of the vegetable garden, chrysanthemum cuttings are growing and are moved into the garden as summer flowers fade. After frost the cycle begins again as new tulips are planted for next spring's flowering.

Spring bulbs are easy because, once planted, most come up year after year except in climates with warm winters. Even tulips, which seldom repeat their first year's opulence, will usually bloom for several years. *BULB POINTERS:* Buy the best quality, order early, plant promptly. If fall planting is delayed, store bulbs in open bags in a well-ventilated, cool place; in the deep South refrigerate if necessary weeks before planting. Set tulips out last, even after Thanksgiving in warm spells, in midwinter in the deep South. Plant all bulbs tip up, twice as deep as they are round, about 3 inches down and 3 inches apart for small bulbs, twice that for larger ones. Plant tulips 7 to 12 inches down if moles, mice, or winter heaving are a problem. Figure on four large bulbs per square foot in a fertile bed. For long life, use one teaspoon bonemeal in the bottom of a bulb's planting hole or one pound per 100-foot row. If soil is stodgy, loosen it with sand or compost. In spring, after a bulb blooms, snap off the energy-sapping seed pod before it can develop. Do not cut foliage until it is yellow and no longer building food reserves.

## THE PLAN

1. Sapling fence along street
2. Grass panel between driveway and rail fence looped with climbing roses and clematis
3. Brick paths
4. Lilies, roses, mixed perennials
5. Roses
6. Peonies and tree roses, some tulips
7. Seasonal beds: tulips in spring; summer-flowering bulbs, and many annuals from seed; chrysanthemums in fall

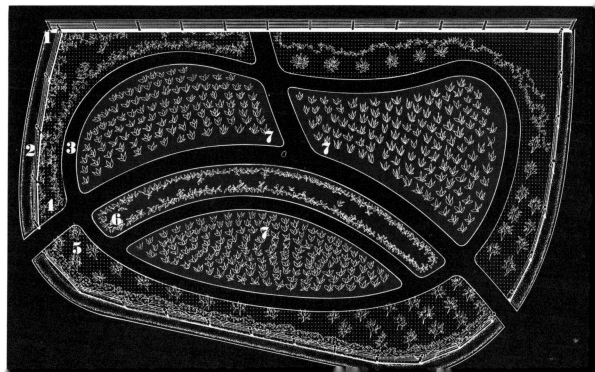

**A summer cottage garden of easy-to-grow flowers and climbing roses**

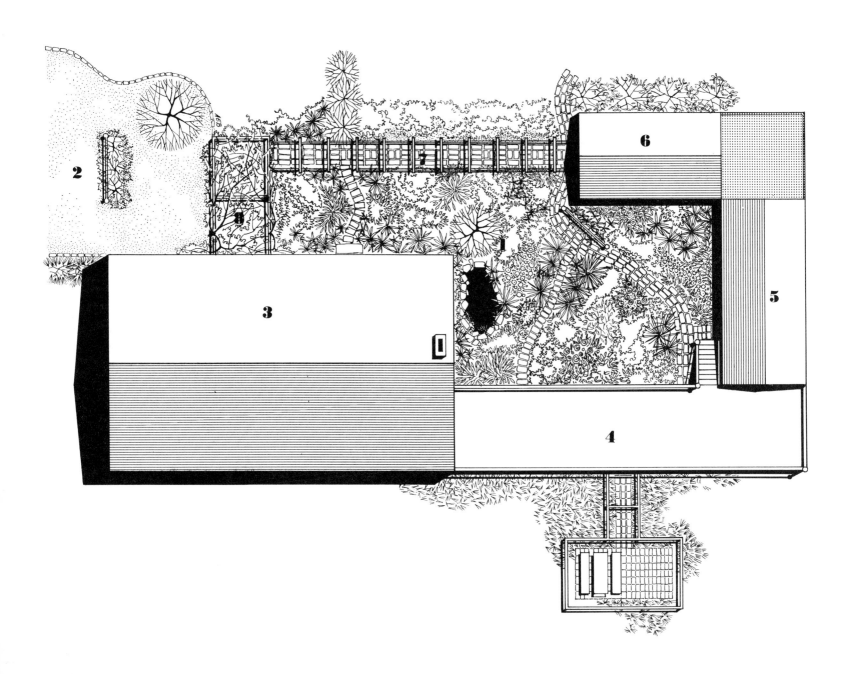

118

## THE PLAN

1. *Flower garden with pool*
2. *Driveway near 1740 barn*
3. *Long Island barn/studio*
4. *New hall/dining area with rooftop sun deck linking barn and other old buildings*
5. *Milkhouse, now kitchen and bedroom*
6. *Crib house, now bedroom*
7. *A 50-foot rose arbor braced against storms by aluminum wire*
8. *Grape arbor completing garden's enclosure*

Robert Dash's house is ringed by wild winds and grass. The garden is protected by a barn and outbuildings, joined by adding a long hall on the windy west and a strong rose arbor on the east. From the stairs and flat roof of the hallway you can see the whole marvelous little garden—the paths made of cinder block garden tiles, a small pool, a profusion of "floppy, easy-to-grow flowers." Mr. Dash makes a point of choosing "lusty flowers that shape up or ship out and that look good even smashed by storms—some root where they fall." Another factor in his success is soil. When remodeling, he set aside the topsoil and put it back well-sifted on top of straw 2 feet thick for richness and drainage. In autumn he adds dried cow manure. He grows twenty-six varieties of day lilies—a jubilation of color all season, pink and red bee balm, yellow-flowered chamomile, and other trouble-free perennials. He also likes rue, alliums, and hybrid thistles, some found through the yearly distribution of the Royal Horticultural Society. He plants these and such annuals as petunias, snapdragons, dusty millers, cosmos, all seemingly at random. "I like to be able to peer over something tall and see something small." Color choice is not random. He likes the way his tall red helenium's "rock and leather shades fade to old muslin." He delights in the counterpoint of burgundy-leaved cardinal flower (*Lobelia cardinalis*) and gray

sage, Dark Opal basil and green zinnias. He likes odd green flowers: Envy zinnias, Irish Eyes rudbeckia, the viridiflora rose. On the rose arbor he grows climbing roses that he chose both for hardiness and color. Some favorites are Lawrence Johnson, Bloomfield Dainty, and Golden Showers (all in shades of yellow); creamy City of York and Bishop Darlington; papery-pink Wind Chimes; and Dortmund with its "reddish petals, creamy buff near the stamens, washing out to a pink beige to almost ivory." Keen sensitivity to his garden's color is reflected in many of his paintings, and in a portfolio of lithographs called *Garden*. "At first you have such exuberance, but I find that intense hues in a small space become tiresome. I am working toward a more muted garden and am ruthless about uprooting if I have made a wrong choice."

### DIGGING A GARDEN POOL

The small shallow pool in this no-lawn garden could be duplicated anywhere. Under a living room window, where the birds it attracts are easily observed, it was scooped out, lined with a foot of coarse peat moss, then plastic sheeting, and a layer of mud. The peat moss cushions the plastic against the danger of tearing if frost should heave a rock from below. Around it, hibiscus, cattails, and wild flags grow, along with clumps of watercress transplanted each year from a stream.

# 17

## A move-around garden that flowers wherever you put it

"Permanence and change are what we gardeners work for," says Enid A. Haupt, whose serene green garden is varied by portable pot plants. A movable garden is her way of always having flowers looking their best and growing their best in and near the house when she is there to enjoy them. "I travel a great deal, and pot plants are easier to use than flower arrangements." She was editor of a magazine when she remodeled this house and systematized her flower growing to provide instant color when and where needed. "Someone once asked me which is my favorite flower, and I realized it was whichever was in my hand at the moment." She turned a boathouse into a potting shed, added a greenhouse, put an opaque skylight in the house that opened it to sunlight. She has also opened the world of gardening to others. At a New York hospital a shed, greenhouse, solarium, and therapy rooms are affectionately dubbed "the garden of Enid." She worked with Mrs. Lyndon Johnson on the National Beautification Committee. A recent gift to the American Horticultural Society helped it establish national headquarters at George Washington's historic River Farm, near Mount Vernon, Virginia. "When I first began gardening I didn't know about horticulture. I just gave my plants a lot of attention and love, as you would do for a human being."

"One of the most enjoyable things in life," Mrs. Haupt says, "is being responsible for plants, but you must never go beyond what you can take care of easily." She tries to limit her time and attention to flexible little gardens in and near the house. "Movable plants in pots can make a house and garden one." She speaks of her plants as "old friends, almost immortal, because we have taken cuttings and cuttings and cuttings. The geraniums, for instance, all began with one plant." Most of her other plants, too, were propagated from greenhouse specimens bought as many as twenty years ago, except for the begonias, which are grown from seed each year, and the ficus trees. "You have such a sense of accomplishment when you see what your hands can do with a flower. Working with plants refreshes your sense of wonder." Mrs. Haupt also feels that "Balance is all, as in everything in life. Nothing must detract from the plant, certainly not a showy cachepot or fabric." She likes well-proportioned terra-cotta or gray containers. On the parquet de Versailles terrace, designed for her by Innocenti-Webel, she has gray furniture "for a view without the distraction of color." In the flower room, a small-scale print is a sunny background for the geraniums, begonias, and other flowers she loves. The same fabric, cut with pinking shears, is used as party tablecloths to fit semicircular plywood tables that can be joined around the tall ficus trees. These ten-year-old trees in heavy 14-inch pots have never needed repotting. Their soil is aerated with an ice pick each spring and fall to give the roots oxygen and keep them in good condition. Some of Mrs. Haupt's other plant-saving ideas are also effort savers.

*WATER* Hanging baskets outdoors in drying air need water daily. To make this simple, she uses a watering wand, a hose attachment with a long angled nozzle. "Much easier than the old-fashioned way of dipping a basket in a pail and hanging it back up still dripping." Even the flower room has a hose and drain for easy care and cleanups. "Individual hand-watering will give you twice as many flowers in the long run."

*AIR* "You can't keep the same plant in the house all the time. Though a draft will kill a flower, good air circulation will make it bloom more beautifully." After three days at their peak indoors in summer, her plants get an outing in semishade. Here they can also be comfortably tended and groomed of faded blossoms or leaves. "All plants need air and humidity. Indoor plants will benefit if foliage is misted by spraying water with an atomizer. This extends the lives of plants. Some people play tennis. I get exercise going around spraying plants with an air mister."

*SOIL* Packaged ingredients sold at garden centers are used because they are lightweight and pest-free. (Another precaution against soil pests is giving plants that have been outdoors a whoosh of ordinary household bug spray twelve hours before bringing them indoors.) For propagating cuttings, a sterile porous mixture of half builder's sand and half perlite is used. Plants are then potted in a formula of half potting soil, half shredded sphagnum, and an added 4-inch pot of nutrients per bushel basket. The sphagnum moss prevents trouble by keeping the soil from getting packed down and waterlogged. Every ten days in good growing weather most of the plants get a balanced fertilizer (15-15-15 or the like); a light dose, diluted with water and thoroughly worked into the soil around the plant, is better than an occasional heavy feeding.

*Good growing practices and easy, watchful care keep this portable garden radiant with flowers and good health.*

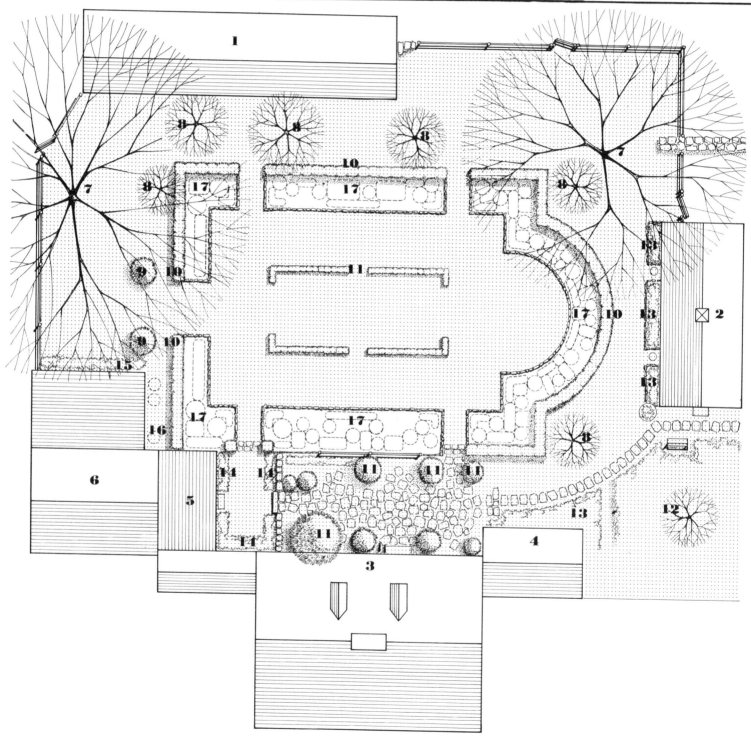

Mr. and Mrs. Charles Akers Bradbury's garden is Colonial in plan but not confined to eighteenth-century plant lists. More than one hundred varieties of perennials grow between the small inner courtyard of boxwood and the dark green frame of yews. A rail fence unites the old buildings, new additions, and the new garden in Westchester County, New York.

*THE PLAN*
*BUILDINGS*
 *1. Open shed*
 *2. Barn, now music room*
 *3. House and stone terrace*
 *4. New studio*
 *5. New screened porch*
 *6. New garage*
*TREES*
 *7. Sugar maple*
 *8. Dogwood*
*SHRUBS*
 *9. Arborvitae*
*10. Yew* (Taxus hicksii)
*11. Boxwood* (Buxus sempervirens suffruticosa)
*12. Lilac*
*FOUNDATION PLANTINGS*
*13. Lavender*
*14. Epimedium*
*15. Sweet Cicely*
*VINES*
*16. Clematis* (Nelly Moser, The President, and C. paniculata)
*Formal beds*
*17. Perennial flowers, foliage*


*THE PLANTS*
*Edging plants and colors*
*Silver Mound artemisia, gray*
*Lamb's ears, gray*
*Sedum album, white*
*Dianthus Beatrix, cameo-pink*
*Phlox* (P. subulata), *pink, white*
*Bellflower* (Campanula), *blue*
*Corner beds at far left*

*The Fairy polyantha rose, pink*
*Purple loosestrife* (Lythrum salicaria)
*Rudbeckia, coneflower* (Echinacea purpurea), *purple-pink*
*Lady's Mantle* (Alchemilla), *light green foliage and flower*
*Side beds and arc*
*Sitka peony, white*
*Lobelia* (L. siphilitica), *blue*
*Rosy Veil baby's breath* (Gypsophila paniculata rosea)
*White Luster Rudbeckia* (Echinacea alba)
*All beds, color in June*
*Bearded iris, 35 varieties* (I. germanica)
*Gas plant* (Dictamnus albus), *white*
*Veronica* (V. teucrium), *blue*
*Coralbells* (Heuchera sanguinea), *light red*
*Phlox* (P. divaricata), *lavender-blue*
*All beds, color in July*
*Japanese iris* (I. kaempferi)
*Astilbe, Peach Blossom*
*Blue salvia* (S. farinacea)
*All beds, color July–August*
*Hybrid day lilies* (Hemerocallis) *for early, mid, and late season, all colors but blue*
*Blue flax* (Linum perenne)
*Coronation Gold yarrow* (Achillea)

Together this couple gave new life to an old house and old land. They started with a 1740 house, an open shed and barn, and two old maples. The land was discouraging. Even the barnyard's topsoil had been sold off before they came. But the rocks they unearthed in digging were used to build their terrace. Envisioning flowers to come, they dug and manured the beds for perennials while restoring and adding to the house. Mr. Bradbury, an architect, built the studio, porch, and garage. He gave all the buildings a silvery-gray stain "to marry the old and new." Now everywhere you look there is a reassuring sense of order, and pleasing combinations of color. This garden in rural New York is "the quiet garden we like, with no sharp drama, no clash of colors." Mrs. Bradbury, a painter, uses soft cameo pink throughout the garden but is cautious about purple-pinks; she groups them in one area. The edgings are gentle grays, blues, cameo, and white. Though she likes lemon yellow on her palette, she prefers chrome yellow as a mixer in the garden. (An example of chrome is Coronation Gold Achillea, a yarrow. It is easy to grow and also keeps its color for winter bouquets if hung to dry in a dim, airy place.) "If a color isn't right," Mr. Bradbury says, "up it comes. At first I thought my wife had put springs on the roots of those flowers." Now that the garden has been established, it seems to take care of itself, almost. "Weeds! You can't tell me weeds don't think," Mrs. Bradbury says. "They always come up next to a plant they resemble." Happily, perennials are prolific, too.

# A weekender's easy-does-it organic hay-mulch vegetable garden

## 19

"On some summer weekends my only job is picking," Harry Rogers says. His site is ideal for vegetables—level, well-drained, sunny. If he fails to get the weekly inch of rain his plants need, he has a hose stretched from a spring. But ease in gardening began for him when he discovered mulching. Any mulch keeps the earth moist, smothers weeds, provides clean walkways. Field hay enriches the soil and seems to baffle insects. He pushes it aside to plant.

*THE PLAN*

1. *Kentucky Wonder pole beans*
2. *Asparagus*
3. *Blue salvia*
4. *Mixed zinnias*
5. *Red zinnias*
6. *White asters*
7. *Lincoln peas*
8. *Sweetpod sugar peas*
9. *China cucumbers*
10. *New Zealand spinach*
11. *Mixed gladioli*
12. *Yellow marigolds*
13. *White gladioli*
14. *Yellow lilies*
15. *Red Cherry tomatoes*
16. *Big Boy tomatoes*
17. *Zucchini Elite summer squash*
18. *Sweet and hot peppers*
19. *Sorrel*
20. *Boston lettuce*
21. *Salad Bowl lettuce*
22. *Golden Acre cabbage*
23. *Swiss chard*
24. *Long Season beets*
25. *Pioneer carrots*
26. *American Flag leeks*
27. *Yellow Sweet Spanish onions*
28. *Ebenezer onions*
29. *Chives*
30. *Flat parsley*
31. *Sage*
32. *Rosemary*
33. *Curly parsley*
34. *Tarragon*
35. *Rhubarb*

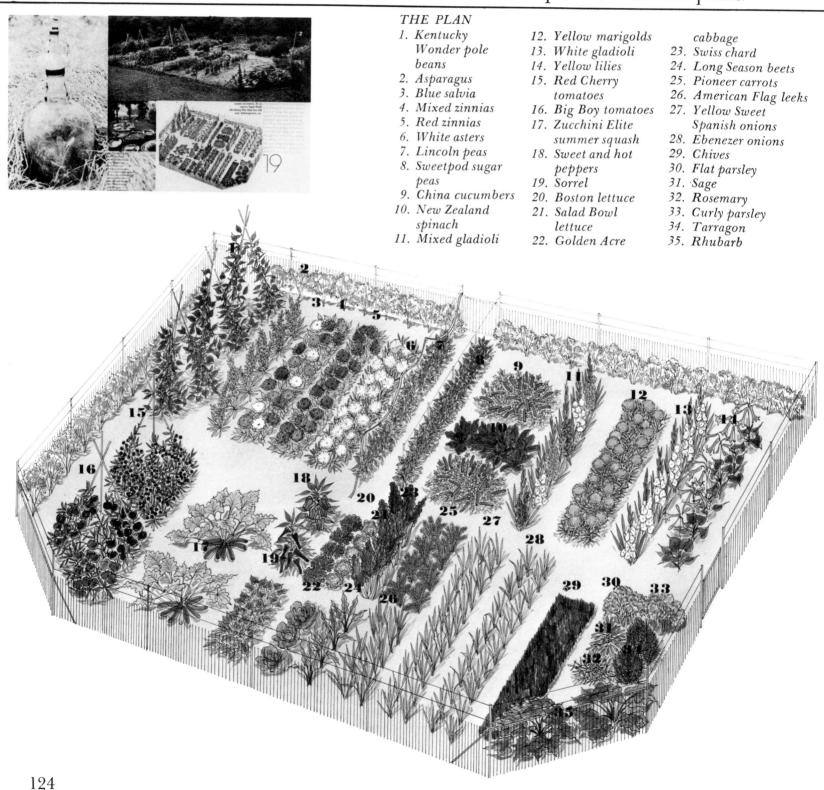

ne mulches merely cover. Or-
nic mulches, like field hay,
dually decompose and im-
ove the soil's texture and fer-
ty. Salt hay is useful but is
wer to decompose than field
y. Once established, a hay-
lched garden does not re-
ire spading, rotary-tilling, or
iting for a man with a plow
ore you can plant. You push
ay the straw where you want
plant or where perennials
d sunshine to wake up.
ds are covered lightly with
soft soil, and rows are then
t open to the light. Harry
gers' inspiration was the book
w to Have a Green Thumb
thout an Aching Back by
th Stout. By trowel and error
has come up with some in-
rations of his own, like the
tomless wine and cider jugs.
over young plants, they work
e miniature greenhouses. Jug
s are taken off on weekends
let the air inside cool off. In
s part of Connecticut frosts
a threat until late May, and
glass cloche makes weekend
dening less risky. After dan-
of frost is past, the gallon
s are retired to the garage
hang by their ears from the
ters. The idea is to collect
dozen or so empties—"my
sts are encouraged to in-
ase the supply"—and simply

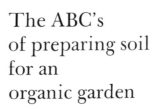

get a local glass cutter to zip off
the bottoms.
Not only jug greenhouses but
easy tepees are helpful in this
garden. To support both pole
beans and tomatoes, tepees are
made of three long-lasting cedar
poles 8 feet long. The poles are
thrust 6 inches into the ground
and bound at the top with cord.
An established organic garden is
so nourishing that it will support more plants than a regu-
lar garden. Flowers and herbs
comfortably share this vegetable
plot, and their general state of
good health is apparent. This,
in part, explains why there are
few bothersome insects. Appar-
ently, too, insects cannot live
comfortably under or in thick
layers of hay, though an un-
mulched garden on the property
had been beseiged. One caution:
In slug country, or in a damp
season you might want to keep
hay at a distance from tender
plants. Slugs—snails without a
shell—can conceal themselves
under soft, decomposing layers.
Mr. Rogers' pests are not insects
and not slugs but canny four-
footed varmints. To protect his
vegetables from rabbits and
woodchucks, he installed a 5-foot
fence with 10 inches of fine-mesh
chicken wire below ground.

## The ABC's of preparing soil for an organic garden

"A good mulch and a fence solve
almost every gardening problem except raccoons," he says.
"These rascals have made me
give up on corn and cantaloupes.
I put a radio out there and had
an all-night talk show going.
They were not fooled. I rigged
up Christmas lights to blink on
and off, and just made it easier
for them to find the best things
to eat, which they promptly did."

*EACH FALL*
*A. Layer of autumn leaves*
*B. Sprinkling of slow-release*
*organic fertilizers as needed*
*C. Layer of field hay (6 inches*
*if you can get enough bales).*
*For the first fall only, Mr.*
*Rogers had a layer of dried cow*
*manure plowed into the*
*earth before adding leaves. For*
*the first three Novembers his*
*organic fertilizers included 100-*
*pound bags each of bonemeal,*
*cotton-seed meal, cotton-seed*
*hull ash, sewage sludge such*
*as Milorganite, and phosphate*
*rock. Now he finds leaves and*
*hay are rich enough. He adds*
*only a 100-pound bag of*
*agricultural lime every third*
*year to counteract leaf acidity.*

*EACH SPRING*
*A. Compost*
*B. Fireplace ashes*
*C. Organic fertilizers*
*When pushing hay aside to*
*plant, Mr. Rogers gives the earth*
*in the open rows a spring*
*tonic. To a wheelbarrow of*
*compost, he adds 3 quarts*
*fireplace ashes and 3 quarts*
*slow-release fertilizers and*
*scatters the mixture as he plants.*
*His compost heap gets every-*
*thing left over from garden or*
*kitchen, including foliage,*
*grass clippings, coffee grounds,*
*eggshells, apple cores, anything*
*except meat scraps. These he*
*puts on the hill for the rac-*
*coons, a gesture more sociable*
*than deterring.*

# 20

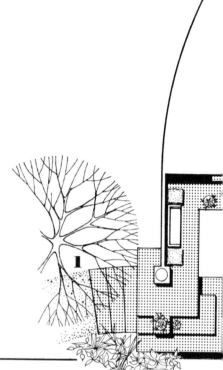

**Pot luck: portable plants for sunny and shady terraces**

Any gardener busy with other work or who must travel as much as Horst P. Horst does can take heart from this photographer's style of gardening: pot luck. When he is at home he makes spur-of-the-moment—but masterful —groupings of his own container plants and what local garden centers can provide. Keeping a blue-and-white color scheme in mind for spring, and a pink-and-red theme for summer, he arranges plants so that his terraces and entry-ways are at their best when he and guests can enjoy them. Like all good gardeners, he uses time away from home to absorb new ideas for more leisurely hours.

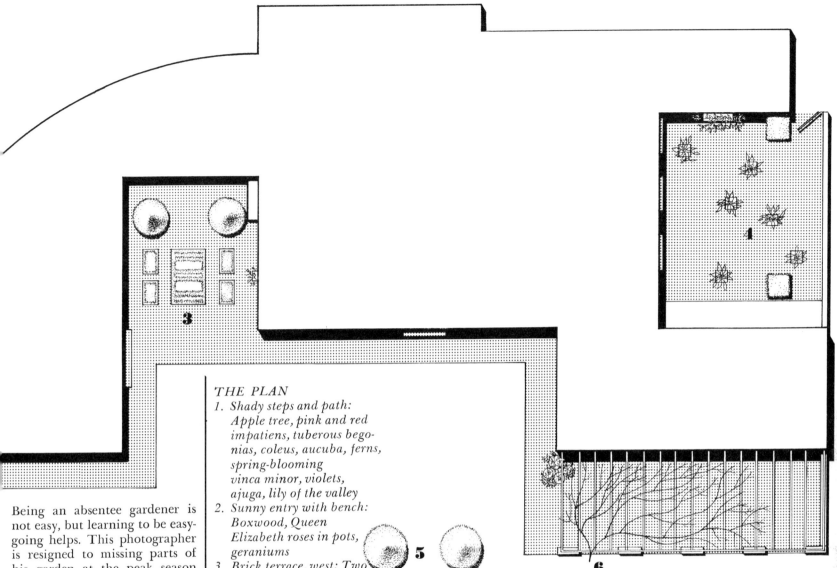

Being an absentee gardener is not easy, but learning to be easygoing helps. This photographer is resigned to missing parts of his garden at the peak season and to making-do. He is equally relaxed about the wildlife that shares his property. He may gently discourage a determined chipmunk from making a home in a geranium pot, but he lets the squirrels steal the apples from the tree by the shady path. "At least there will be no falling apples to damage the coleus plants or impatiens I like so much." Mr. Horst enjoys the wild area around his house and can enjoy the more tailored house area by keeping it simple and spontaneous.

## THE PLAN

1. *Shady steps and path:*
   *Apple tree, pink and red*
   *impatiens, tuberous bego-*
   *nias, coleus, aucuba, ferns,*
   *spring-blooming*
   *vinca minor, violets,*
   *ajuga, lily of the valley*
2. *Sunny entry with bench:*
   *Boxwood, Queen*
   *Elizabeth roses in pots,*
   *geraniums*
3. *Brick terrace, west: Two*
   *yews; four small beds*
   *of blue Wabash iris,*
   *forget-me-nots and*
   *portulaca; a center herb*
   *bed; a pink Blossom*
   *Time climbing rose*
4. *Brick courtyard, east:*
   *Irregular potting holes*
   *for tulips or primula in*
   *spring, gloxinia or*
   *sedums in summer,*
   *chrysanthemums in fall,*
   *Royal Gold climbing rose*
5. *Sunny grass terrace:*
   *Alberta spruces (slow-*
   *growing, never need clip-*
   *ping) in painted boxes*
6. *Slatted pergola: House*
   *plants out for summer.*
   *Hanging baskets of*
   *petunias, ivy-leaf*
   *geraniums, tuberous*
   *begonias. Nursery-grown*
   *flowers in pots. Concord*
   *grape, morning glory,*
   *and moonflower vines.*

## SUMMER VINES

*Though many people chip*
*or soak morning glory*
*(Ipomea) and moonflower*
*(Calonyction) seeds*
*before planting, Mr. Horst*
*does not. But he has another*
*tip: Set a row of tiny nails*
*at the top of a wall or*
*pergola, tie thin strings*
*around them, and let them*
*drop to ground level. Leave*
*a few inches at the*
*bottom to tie around a stick*
*or small stone. Bury these*
*in the soil as you plant,*
*and the vines will have an*
*invisible pathway to climb*
*to the top.*

127

## A perfectionist's small round gardens and green-thumb pot-plant ideas

A series of small linked gardens planted decade by decade by the J. Liddon Pennock, Jrs., is now a green mansion of intimate outdoor rooms. A round garden, their first, adjoins a stone dining terrace. The next rondel has a lily pool. The ivy on the steps linking them was not trained. It grew from the sides,

covered the risers, and only the treads are clipped. An innovative florist, Mr. Pennock is a perfectionist other perfectionists consult on matters ranging from house plants to White House party and Christmas decorations. At Mr. and Mrs. Pennock's house, north of Philadelphia, every room is a garden of pot plants and every garden is a room, with space for outdoor entertaining, and small corners of delight.

Every room always seems ready for a party at the Pennocks' "Meadowbrook Farm." The house abounds with hanging baskets, tall flowering standards, ivy and rosemary trained as topiary. Everything reflects one of Mr. Pennock's basic principles, "Good grooming is a prerequisite to successful gardening." Pruning is a favorite chore. *THE ROUND GARDENS* have evergreen walls of holly, rhododendron, laurel, weeping hemlock, even English ivy that clambers up the bare trunks of tall white pines. A long axis forms a vista now stretching from a small gazebo beyond a kitchen garden, through the original round gardens, on to a swimming-pool pavilion. Yet you perceive this grand-scale triumph only when you stand at the heart of each intimate, seemingly self-contained area. Mr. Pennock believes, "No garden should be seen in its entirety from one vantage point. There should always remain an element of surprise as one proceeds from section to section, room to room." His advice to anyone just starting a garden is, "Don't submerge a house in what is erroneously called foundation planting. Consider the growth potential and controllability of your shrubs and trees." He also encourages young people to learn the thrifty skills that can propagate many plants from one: "Three years ago we had just one miniature euonymous plant; now it has become six fine low hedges." Another bit of advice: "Remember that what is planted in the cool exhilarating spring must be maintained in the hot enervating summer. Plant what you will enjoy."

*POT PLANTS* are used outdoors and indoors. The Pennocks' greenhouse is now open to the public, and house plants and containers are sold "partly to help maintain all this" and because Mr. Pennock thoroughly enjoys collecting and growing and teaching new gardeners how to care for his plants' offspring. "An ideal climate for plants in pots," he says, "is a copper tray with one-fourth inch of water in pebbles one inch deep." To keep up the humidity, he recommends misting most house plants daily. He is not adverse to insecticides, if needed, but suggests rotenone or other organic sprays. One of his rules startles some growers: "Underfeed but feed continually." With every watering he gives his pot plants a balanced fertilizer, more diluted than usually suggested for periodic feedings. Mr. Pennock likes plastic pots for hanging plants because they are lightweight and do not dry out as quickly as clay, but he finds the common white or harsh green colors unpleasing. To make them nearly invisible, he sprays them with flat black paint, adds moss-green paint, and rubs with cheesecloth to blend. When he buys a contemporary cement planter or figure, he sponges on dark brown cement paint, then light brown, and rubs it almost off for a soft, weathered look. Every clay pot or container of any sort is immaculate. In the greenhouse new pots are washed with a disinfectant. Cuttings are started in flats of sterile perlite and peat moss. When plants are transferred to pots, they grow in this formula: one-third sterilized soil and two-thirds vermiculite, perlite, peat moss, sand, and charcoal, all balanced according to the plant's particular needs.

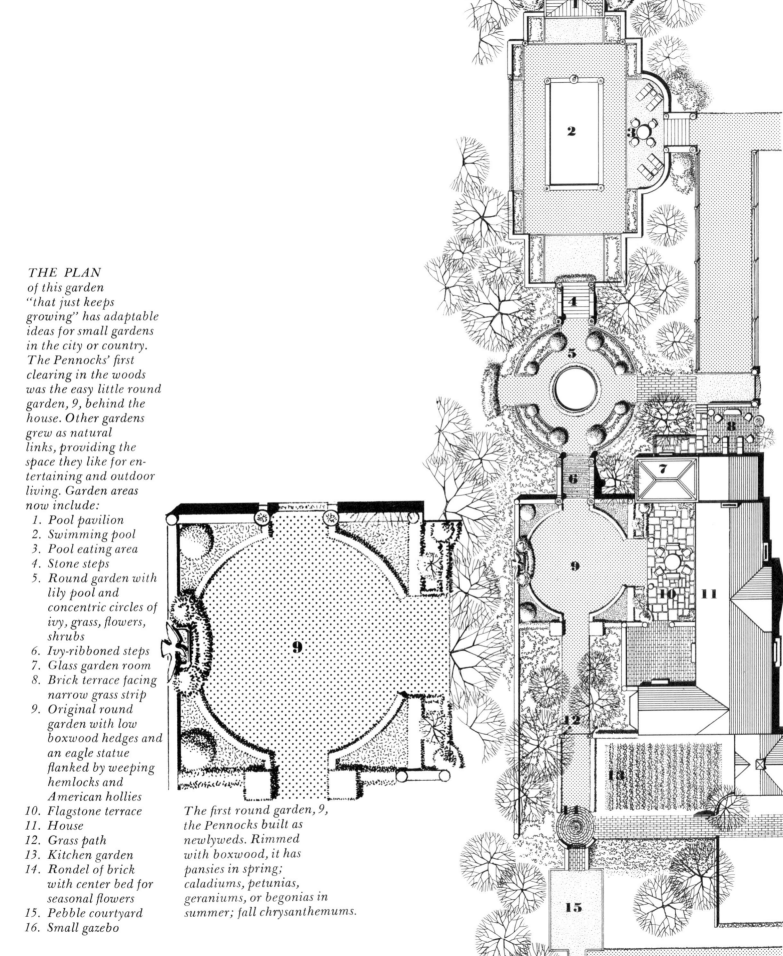

**THE PLAN**
of this garden
"that just keeps
growing" has adaptable
ideas for small gardens
in the city or country.
The Pennocks' first
clearing in the woods
was the easy little round
garden, 9, behind the
house. Other gardens
grew as natural
links, providing the
space they like for en-
tertaining and outdoor
living. Garden areas
now include:

1. Pool pavilion
2. Swimming pool
3. Pool eating area
4. Stone steps
5. Round garden with
   lily pool and
   concentric circles of
   ivy, grass, flowers,
   shrubs
6. Ivy-ribboned steps
7. Glass garden room
8. Brick terrace facing
   narrow grass strip
9. Original round
   garden with low
   boxwood hedges and
   an eagle statue
   flanked by weeping
   hemlocks and
   American hollies
10. Flagstone terrace
11. House
12. Grass path
13. Kitchen garden
14. Rondel of brick
    with center bed for
    seasonal flowers
15. Pebble courtyard
16. Small gazebo

*The first round garden, 9,
the Pennocks built as
newlyweds. Rimmed
with boxwood, it has
pansies in spring;
caladiums, petunias,
geraniums, or begonias in
summer; fall chrysanthemums.*

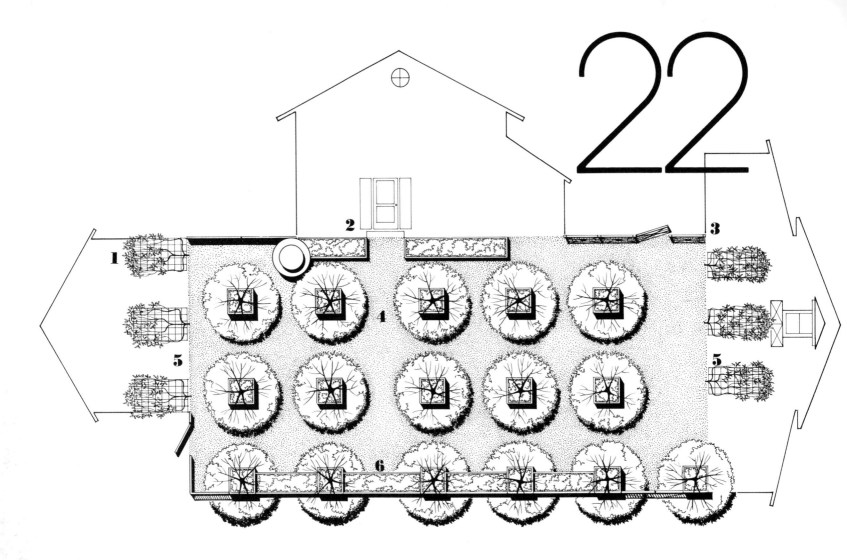

**A miniature orchard and berry garden in boxes for easy care**

Old World grace pervades this garden, set in a cluster of remodeled farm buildings and furnished with a thatched dovecote, straw beehives, herb beds by a bedroom door. It was also planned for efficient use of time and footage. Six espaliered fruit trees hug the walls. Sixteen dwarf fruit trees in boxes permit Mrs. Quaintance Mason to do her own pruning, spraying, harvesting. The trees' boxes, open at the bottom, double as beds for strawberries, and one row, linked by long boxes for raspberries, lines a picket fence.

Until a few years ago this transplanted bit of France in rural New York was a huddle of barns, sheepfolds, sheds, pony stalls, and a kennel for forty greyhounds. Half-timbered stucco covers the siding of the buildings that were preserved. Near the entrance is a very old sugar maple. The silo-like design of the kitchen wing was inspired by turrets in a Norman village. Two barns, now a house and garage, and a pony stall, now a daughter's house, frame a courtyard that became an orchard pretty in all seasons.

*THE PLAN*
1. *Barn/garage*
2. *Barn/house*
3. *Stall/house*
4. *Orchard—sixteen dwarf apple, pear, peach, and crabapple trees, underplanted with strawberries, in earth-filled redwood boxes*
5. *Espaliered trees trained flat on 9-by-14-foot frames*
6. *Raspberries in four narrow boxes forming part of a fence*

*The strawberries are fraises des bois, the true wild strawberry that fruits most of the summer. They are the French variety, Charles V, and the Russian variety, Catherine the Great. The raspberries along the picket fence separating the gravel courtyard and meadow are the large Indian Summer variety. The espaliered fruit trees are Yellow Delicious apples flanked by Bartlett pears.*

*DWARF FRUIT TREES* are handy for one person to plant, prune, spray, harvest. And one can expect full-size fruit in about three years instead of waiting five to ten years. Grafted on dwarfing rootstock, these fruit trees grow 5 to 10 feet tall, not 30 as standard apples, pears, and cherries do. A dwarf fruit tree needs only 10 feet of root space between itself and its neighbor. Ten mature dwarf fruit trees need no more spreading room than one ordinary apple tree at maturity. For cross-pollination, most fruit trees need a partner of a different variety within 50 feet, for example a McIntosh apple and a Delicious apple. Peach trees are self-fruitful, so even the smallest garden can have just one of these. Always plan a miniature orchard first on paper, then by sight and tape measure. To plant:

1. *DIG A HOLE* roughly 6 to 8 inches wider and deeper than the root ball or bare roots. Put the turned-up soil on burlap or a piece of plastic to protect surrounding lawn or gravel. Keep topsoil and less porous subsoil in separate piles.
2. *ENRICH THE SUBSOIL* pile with one-third quantity of peat moss, then mingle it with the topsoil pile. To the total, add a half shovelful of planting formula fertilizer (4-10-6) or rich compost. Fill roughly one-third of the hole with this mixture.
3. *PLANT TREE* in hole after removing it from container. Lift the tree by its trunk to center it, and spread the roots downward and outward. Use the remaining enriched soil to fill the hole. Pack well or wash the soil down with water to avoid air pockets around the roots.
4. *CHECK THE GRAFT UNION,* the knob between the trunk and roots, to be sure that it is set above ground. If the tree is set too low, the trunk itself might form roots and the tree could revert to nondwarfing characteristics.
5. *WATER THOROUGHLY.* Make a rim of earth around the hole and pour in one bucket of water or more. Thereafter be sure the tree gets 1 inch of watering or rainfall each week during the growing seasons.

To keep trees healthy, a periodic spraying program is usually necessary. In early spring before the buds swell, use a dormant oil spray to kill overwintering insects that will damage the tree itself. Before and after flowering, use a multipurpose fruit-tree spray. Prune when dormant to keep branches open and strong.

131

What began as the Josiah H. Child, Jrs.', weekend salad patch is now as exciting to the children, Jo, Mars, and Suzy, as to the parents. Each area can be separately cultivated, is flexible, manageable in size, and pretty. The patches are bordered by pine-chip paths and flowers chosen to harmonize in color with vegetables, their blossoms, and foliage.

*THE PLAN*

1. *The gate in a fence purple with grapes opens to a path edged with lavender-blue ageratum; Concord grapes*
2. *Path parallel to rows of Ozark Beauty and Sparkle strawberries*
3. *Purple and white sweet alyssum edging rows of Dark Opal basil, purple eggplant, flowering cabbage, beets, beans, Chinese cabbage, leeks, shallots, dill*
4. *Fork in path around original patch, "our salad bowl," of mixed herbs and lettuce (Oak Leaf, Bibb, Cos) now edged by nasturtiums*
5. *French marigolds edging flowering kale, Nantes carrots, okra, eggplant, leeks*
6. *Green basil bordering bright red peppers and tomatoes*
7. *Red zinnias edging witloof chicory (Belgian endive), parsnips, and salsify*
8. *Red zinnias edging corn rows*
9. *Rhubarb, also red*
10. *Red raspberries by rail fence*
11. *Rutabagas, white turnips*
12. *Katahdin potatoes, two beds*
13. *Cucumbers and zucchini*

All annuals are grown from seed except tomatoes, peppers, and eggplant, which need a longer season than the Childs' New England coastland provides. Cool-weather spring crops, such as edible pea pods, spinach, Swiss chard, and scallions, preceded summer and fall crops in plan. Melons, squash grow outside fence.

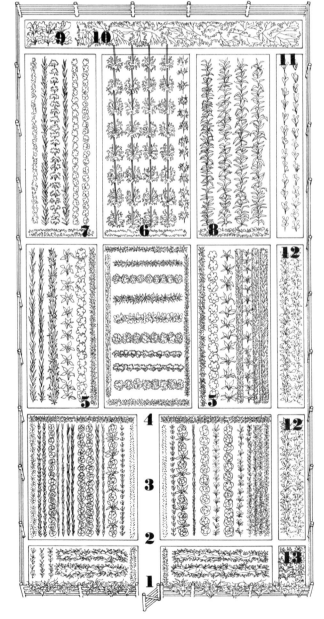

*Even the children study seed catalogues and help pick varieties to suit their own culinary specialty. To have meal-size harvests and great variety, many crops are sown successively—sow a row, wait a week, sow again. This keeps picking easy-going, too. Rabbits were a menace, but now a cedar fence has aluminum mesh extended 8 inches underground —a bafflement to Peter Rabbit but a relief to the gardeners.*

Because Ralph Du Casse's lot sloped steeply toward the back, the 32-by-40-foot area needed a retaining wall and additional soil. Too narrow for machinery, the leveling was done by "skinny men with skinny wheelbarrows." Too shady for grass, the surface was paved with brick. Trees were planted along a fence to shut out neighbors in the nicest sort of way.

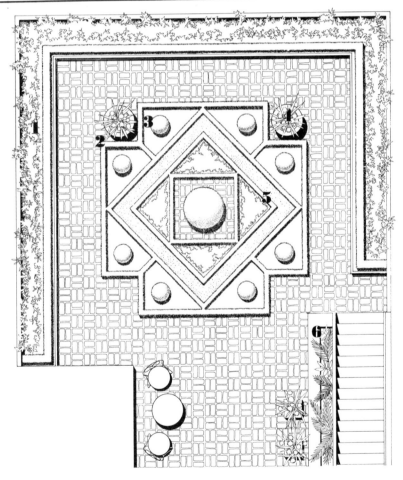

In this garden of green shrubs, trees, and ivy borders, all the flowers are white. White azaleas, rhododendrons (mild climate hybrid Mrs. A. T. De La Mare), French marguerites, shasta daisies, tuberous begonias, chrysanthemums, and other flowering plants all grow in containers. Some catch fleeting sun near the deep shade of the porch overhang. Tuberous begonias thrive in baskets hanging from the porch rafters. Some of the flowers are awaiting their moment of glory in the urns on plinths at two corners of the boxwood parterre. The white lily of the Nile, a tuber, will stay in bloom for six to eight weeks. A less dedicated gardener could easily buy nursery plants in season, but Mr. Du Casse brings his own to their peak. Still, this is an easy-upkeep formal garden, and in San Francisco's moist, gentle air outdoor container plants usually need watering only once a week. Chamomile, the perennial herb that grows in the center triangles of the parterre, stays green three seasons. The pittosporum trees, a house plant in colder areas, have been specially pruned so that their branches interweave to form a pleached evergreen border, a ruff at the top of the lattice fence. Landscape architect: Charles Deaton.

*THE PLAN*

1. *Pittosporum (P. undulatum) and English ivy by fence*
2. *Boxwood hedges (Buxus sempervirens suffruticosa)*
3. *Boxwood spheres*
4. *Urns with lily of the Nile (Agapanthus africanus albus)*
5. *Chamomile (Anthemis nobilis)*
6. *Tree ferns (Alsophila australis)*

133

**25** More by far than most gardens can offer is compressed in painter Barbara Cagiati Draper's backyard—organically grown fruits, flowers, herbs, vegetables, berries, grapes, and shade trees to sit under to view the gardens and green

## An organic backyard farm of fruit trees, vegetables, and flowers

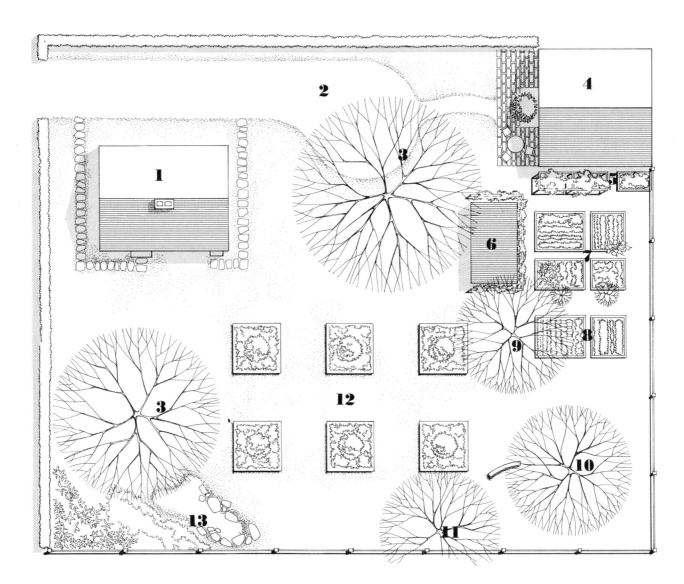

lawn. She takes care of everything herself, and her paintings are often inspired by her garden. In a grassy area that gets sun most of the day, she set out a miniature orchard of six dwarf fruit trees in little 8-foot flower gardens. Each is rimmed and raised by railway ties, and the size is "not too long or wide or inaccessible for easy planting, weeding, and picking." The dwarf apples, peaches, and pears will remain small enough to prune and harvest without ever lugging a ladder, and the orchard doubles as a strolling garden.

### THE PLAN
1. House
2. Driveway and privet hedge
3. Silver maple
4. Barn-studio
5. Compost bins hidden by arbor of Concord and Niagara grapes
6. Pump house/tool shed
7. Vegetables, flowers, beach plum, blueberries
8. Herbs and flowers
9. Mimosa, silk tree (Albizzia julibrissin)
10. Pin oak and bench
11. Standard-size apple tree
12. Six fruit trees with flowers, herbs
13. Fishpond near border of white pines and Japanese black pines

The key organic-gardening principles practiced here are: using no chemical fertilizers or sprays, enriching the earth with composted refuse from kitchen and garden, and encouraging birds and growing certain plants that are natural enemies of plant-destroying pests. "I am gardening more and more in the organic way," this Long Island gardener says. "In the past I used chemical fertilizers. Now I put homemade compost and cow manure on the beds, and I've noticed a difference. Every plant keeps its own character. Small plants are not forced to be superplants, and the color, I find, is superior. Pests have practically disappeared. The only spray I use is the dormant oil variety, to prevent leaf curl in pears. I plant flowers in among the vegetables, and they help each other. It has been proved that certain plants repell insects—nasturtiums, onions, garlic, leeks. Marigolds deter nematodes. Birds are also helpful to me in the garden. Sparrows will eat slugs. To keep weeds down I use wood chips and sugar cane between rows of vegetables."

### A GOOD GARDENER'S TIPS
*WATER* Fruits and vegetables need 1 inch of water or rainfall weekly. She does two jobs in one. Watering the sunny fruit and flower gardens with a rotating sprinkler also takes care of the grass most exposed to sun. The rest of the lawn is shady and can take care of itself.

*SOIL* She adds cow manure to beds in winter, compost and manure in spring, bonemeal and ground limestone as needed. She avoids planting the same vegetables in the same spot each year.

*PESTS* Saucers of beer placed under foliage attract and drown greedy slugs. A barrier of shingles stuck in the ground around vegetables protects them from cutworms and daunts rabbits.

*FRUIT TREES* Pruning with sharp secateurs lets sunshine in for healthy fruit. Leaving a foot of free space around tree trunks is also healthful, whether underplanted with grass or flowers.

### FRUITS AND FLOWERS
Each dwarf fruit tree is underplanted with bulbs that come up every spring, some when the trees themselves are small clouds of bloom.
There are snowdrops, chionodoxa, crocus, grape hyacinths, miniature iris, Kaufmanniana tulips.
In summer the beds are mixed bouquets of roses (one bush per bed), perennials, and shallow-rooted annuals that are easy to plant over bulbs. Blue salvia and lobelia, white nicotiana and yellow marguerites are in some of the little gardens. Dwarf marigolds are added late and bloom right through fall.
In winter bushy heathers, evergreen candytuft, gray santolina, sage, and artemisias give form and texture. In the sketch is an Elberta peach with some of the summer flowers:

1. Rose bush
2. Ageratum
3. Petunias
4. Violas
5. Nasturtiums
6. Dianthus
7. Gaillardia
8. Snapdragons
9. Verbena

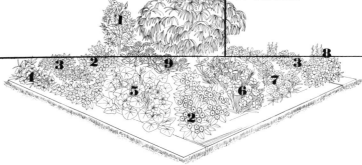

This "lazy garden" required hard thinking to avoid hard work. "We'll have our carpet and its holes for maybe ten years," George R. Numrich, Jr., says, "so we planned it first on paper, rolled out the carpet, and marked it with chalk and a soft pencil to see exactly how the plan worked before we cut." They weighed down this permanent mulch with rocks—"Carpet takes a while to flatten and become one with the earth"—and now it seems downright indigenous.

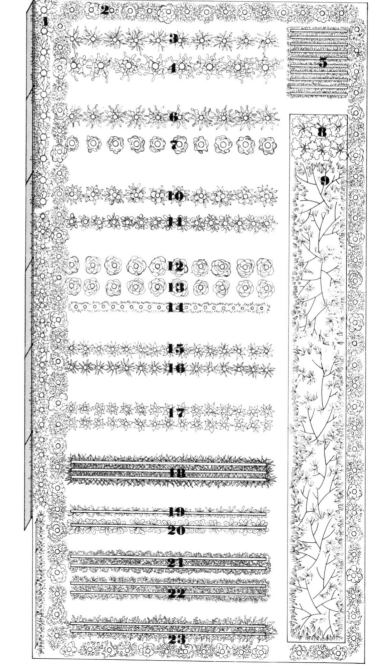

This vegetable garden is 28 by 46 feet. Paths are 2 feet wide. It required two lengths of 12-foot carpet. Narrow strips edge open bed for perennial rhubarb and asparagus.

THE PLAN
 1. Wire fence to support ten tomato plants, twenty cucumbers, twenty pea plants
 2. Borders of marigolds, ornamental kale and cabbage, with sunflowers at the corners
 3. Saint Pat scallop squash
 4. Zucchini
 5. Mixed herbs
 6. Brussels sprouts
 7. Cauliflower
 8. Rhubarb
 9. Asparagus, bordered at times by beans
10. Broccoli
11. Eggplant
12. Red cabbage
13. Cabbage
14. Celery
15. Lima beans
16. Peppers
17. String beans
18. Onions
19. Salsify
20. Spinach
21. Mixed lettuce
22. Carrots
23. Radishes

The George R. Numrich, Jrs., bought unbacked outdoor carpeting and used a 3-inch circular saw attachment on a hand drill to make holes in it for planting. A sharp knife makes slits for root crops that can get too plump to pry out of a 3-inch hole. Bricks and stones hold the carpet down. Digging is done with a trowel or spoon. Extra soil is deposited in a tray. A broom or vacuum sweeps up spills. "Of course I was worried, as most people would be, that my carpet idea would be terribly expensive," Mr. Numrich says. "But if you make it clear to the carpet dealer that you want a twelve-foot roll to cart away, not to have fitted and installed, the cost is less than you would expect. We used Armstrong polypropylene carpet from the Ensign do-it-yourself line, less than three dollars a square yard. Our garden paid for itself the first year, figuring two dollars an hour for the weeding we *didn't* do. It has also survived a cold upstate New York winter and was ready for planting weeks earlier than any other gardens here. We also used to have to rotary-till every year. With a second-year carpet garden, a few turns in each hole with the hand drill and an L-rod attachment, and you're ready in minutes. Carpet also gives vegetables the old zap. We started this garden Memorial Day, and by mid-July the crop was feeding the family. Our eggplant yield is about twenty-five per bush. Carpet gardens also get very few insects. Why I cannot say, unless most insects live or rest in the ground, and newcomers can't get down and residents can't get up." After carpeting and automating their no-work garden, George and Fran Numrich, you might think, could consign their garden tools to cobwebs. Not so. The time they save on their vegetable garden does give them more time for tennis and swimming, but like all true gardeners, they have still other ideas up their garden sleeves. They are making a garden that . . . but that's another story. Their word, and ours, to fellow gardeners is: "Experiment —and keep it easy."

# INDEX